Winning Business in the Property Sector

Techniques to maximise personal sales effectiveness

Patrick Forsyth

2006

EG Books

A division of Reed Business Information

Estates Gazette
1 Procter Street, London WC1V 6EU

©Patrick Forsyth, 2006

ISBN 0 7282 0488 6

Typeset in Palatino 10/12 by Amy Boyle, Rochester
Printed by Bell & Bain Ltd, Glasgow

"God is on the side not of the heavy battalions, but of the best shots."
Voltaire

Dedication

For Grant Wisby, who kindly surveyed the manuscript for this book as carefully as he surveys everything else — many thanks.

Contents

Part 5 Afterword — the Way Ahead

Acknowledgements

As always with the management books I have written, it would be impossible to present any useful information without the stimulus of those I have worked with in many ways — clients, colleagues, contacts of all sorts — over the years. Conducting training is especially useful as the dialogue created works in both directions. I am grateful for everything that comes this way whether wittingly or unwittingly provided.

This book began with a conversation at a conference, when a business friend and collaborator met the publisher. So thanks to Frances Kay for her effective networking and for thinking of me for this one (her own book, on communication in the property world, is also published by EG books and is to be recommended). My work in this sector goes much further back: when the professions first opened up and began to take an interest in marketing I worked first in the accountancy sector. With the publication of my book *Marketing Professional Services* (the latest edition of which is published by Kogan Page), this rapidly expanded into other professional services, including many in the world of property.

Thanks are due to many people with whom I have crossed paths along the way and who have stimulated my thinking; and to Alison Richards and her colleagues at EG Books for their confidence in putting these thoughts into print and presenting them in such a well-designed format.

Last, but not least, special thanks to Grant Wisby, of Chartered Surveyors Shreeves, are recorded in the dedication.

Preface

"Everyone lives by selling something."

Robert Louis Stevenson

The property world is a special one. Many businesses and different types of expertise contribute to it. These range from those who design and build property to those who help maintain it. Specifically, it includes: architects, surveyors, planning consultants, land agents, managing agents and estate agents together with others such as property lawyers and some linked to financial services.

Each and every one of them has this in common: they must ensure that they have a sufficient number of clients, willing to pay a sufficient amount of money for products and/or services that they are competent to supply, ranged over time to allow their business to be manageable and profitable. Realistically, that means that they must engage in a process to generate business. The umbrella term for this is marketing, and a variety of promotional techniques are involved in it. Some of this involves few people — sometimes, in a small business, just one. But it also involves the individual process of communicating persuasively on an individual basis to relate to specific individuals and organisations and win their business; someone in the business has to sell. Indeed, in a business of any size a number of people have to sell and must do so effectively.

Although part of the marketing mix, selling is sometimes overshadowed by more complex or fashionable techniques and can thus sometimes be regarded as a poor relation of marketing.

It is in no way any such thing.

Selling is a vital strategic and tactical part of the marketing mix, and in many areas of the property sector it is the final link in the marketing chain between an organisation and its clients. In such cases, however well implemented other aspects of the marketing mix may be, they achieve nothing if the quality of execution of personal professional selling is not of a high order. It is this selling that converts the interest generated by other promotional communications into actual business.

Perhaps nowhere is selling more likely to be underestimated than when the "product" is a service. Sometimes it is felt that a service speaks for itself, and that no selling is necessary. Sometimes, especially in small businesses, the people involved are experts in the delivery of the service, selling is not their stock in trade, indeed sometimes too overt a sales role is seen as diluting the image the firm is at pains to present and the professional relationship the individual wants.

Note: In some organisations in the property world the word "selling" may conjure up an image of a hard sell, "pushy" approach that is unlikely to be compatible with professional client relationships. Be assured that the word is used here with an understanding that such an approach would be wholly inappropriate; selling here means professional selling in a style that is acceptable, helps build relationships and increases the chances of securing business.

An essential process

Yet, in every case selling, actively winning business is essential. What is being sold may vary. As has been said, such includes the services of an architect, a surveyor or planner and the whole plethora of advice and services they offer; the property (of all sorts) handled by an estate agent and many more. Much of this might be categorised within the sector of professional services: those selling professional and technical services on a fee basis and includes a range of people from accountants to lawyers, some of whom also work in the property sector. All this overlaps into financial services, which again encompasses a range of different things from banking to insurance and more.

Selling is a social skill. It is a communications skill. And, as anyone who has been involved in a breakdown of communications knows, communicating clearly — *but you didn't say that!* — is not guaranteed to be easy. In selling the communication must:

- inform — and do so clearly
- persuade
- differentiate.

All three are important and thus selling must be done right, with techniques and approaches being deployed with appropriate precision.

Not rocket science

Selling involves a variety of approaches and techniques. It is not rocket science, nor is it unmanageably intellectually taxing. But it is complex. There is a great deal going on in the interaction and a lot to bear in mind for those trying to do it well. The complexity comes from the need to deploy skills appropriately, keep all the balls in the air and maximise the chances of success throughout the process.

Three other things are vital:

- *Selling is a bespoke activity*: there is no one right way to sell property services, or anything else for that matter. It is not a question of scripting the approach or going about things by rote. Effective selling is deployed client-by-client, day-by-day and meeting-by-meeting. It is what works for a particular circumstance today. Tomorrow, certainly next week or next year, something a little different will be necessary.
- *Services are different*: many of the businesses at which this book is directed are services, some specialist professional services. This is assumed in the text; here the one overall thing to take on board is that services are not, by their nature, testable. In selling a service, confidence and belief must be engendered so that the prospective client can be prompted to take action even though it often means committing to paying out money, and only later finding out if their chosen supplier is any good or not.
- *Selling is a fragile process*: success, to a large extent, is in the details. One seemingly small matter omitted or handled inappropriately can result in rejection. Something done especially well (matching this client especially well) can make a disproportionate and positive difference. You need to keep on your toes and be quick on your feet.

I can probably type as well now as I ever will (not perfectly, but fast enough for the writing I do). Provided I continue to type regularly my skills will be maintained, and unless the "querty" keyboard is replaced no further learning will be necessary. Selling is not like that. We can all spend a lifetime learning to sell. It is a dynamic skill and must be applied appropriately "on the day". Even then success is not guaranteed, no one wins them all — the best technique maximises strike rate and that is as much as can be hoped for.

Selling was never easy. Today, in competitive and dynamic property markets, it can be damned difficult; certainly it demands a considered and professional approach. Selling intangible services, a prevailing theme of this book, presents special problems and demands specific approaches. It is these that this book examines. There is no magic formula that guarantees sales success (although I must have been asked what the secret is on every sales training course I have ever conducted). However, there are some things — of which more anon — which have a particularly strong impact, but one thing acts as a necessary foundation: that is the view taken of the process by whoever is doing the selling. To put that in context, let me say that — based on my observation and experience — the most successful people in selling are those who take the trouble to understand how the process works. They work at deploying the techniques in the best possible way in the light of that understanding.

Here we review a variety of aspects of the specific task of selling successfully as it applies to those working in the property sector. Such a review cannot guarantee success, but it could help put you in a position where you can succeed.

The message that follows is addressed primarily to the person doing the selling. This includes those from full-time dedicated field sales people to those who must sell as part of other, perhaps senior, professional and consultative jobs, including the consultant and the general manager. In many cases, the person is technically qualified — an architect or surveyor say — and must posses persuasive communication, and all that goes with it, as additional skills if they are to succeed in their total task.

A final introductory point: terminology varies, but most people likely to read this talk of "clients" rather than "customers", and the first word thus appears most here. So, let us see how you can turn prospects into clients and clients into loyal clients who buy from you again and again.

Patrick Forsyth
Touchstone Training & Consultancy
28 Saltcote Maltings, Maldon, Essex CM9 4QP, UK
January 2006

Part 1

The New Realities of the Sales Role

"Dealing with customers takes knowledge, time and patience — after all, if sales people don't have that, they should look for another line of work."
Lee Iacocca (former CEO of Chrysler Motors)

Introduction

"The meek shall inherit the earth, but they'll never increase market share."
William McGowan

The selling process in context

Selling — the personal interaction between buyer and seller — is a key part of the overall marketing process. In many businesses, including property, it is essentially the final link. In other words, whatever other marketing activity has been undertaken, from sending a brochure or mailing to running a major advertising campaign, and however much interest it has generated, selling must convert that interest — turning it into action to buy.

That said, it is worth emphasising that selling is only as good as the organisation that supports it; many different people contribute not only to an organisation's image but to the service it offers. Sales people — and, in this sector, exactly who that is may range widely — must use excellence in both these areas as a foundation to what they do, any shortfall in these areas inevitably affects how well they can perform.

Sometimes the sales process consists of a single event — you talk to the client and, all being well, they buy. On other occasions, the nature of the product and a client's attitude to it mean that a whole series of events must take place. These range from a simple enquiry to a series of meetings and more besides (sending a written proposal or making a presentation, for instance). All of this is important and whatever is done it must be done well; the focus here is primarily on the face-to-face interaction between sales people and clients.

3

The sales task is to communicate clearly and persuasively, and very often to *differentiate* an offering from that of competition. It is a fragile process, by which I mean that results can be changed — for good or ill — by small variations in approach. This may even be down to the use of one word rather than another, certainly to one description or another. Markets may be competitive, clients demanding and fickle, and selling success will not "just happen" because you have a good product or the "gift of the gab". As has been said, in today's market a key issue is to differentiate, to ensure your approach sets you apart from competition. But of one thing you can be sure:

Selling success can be made more certain if you adopt an active approach, understand the way it works and deploy the correct techniques in the right way.

Think about any skill. Can you juggle with three flaming torches without burning holes in the carpet? No? Maybe not, but there are people who can. What is the difference between them and you? Perhaps only that they have thought about how to do it, understood how to go about it and then practised doing it. Selling is no different.

The archetypal "born salesman" is rare. People who are good at selling, however, are much more common. And the best of them have a secret. They understand the process of buying and selling. They adopt a conscious approach in the light of that understanding, and they deploy an approach that uses well-chosen techniques that are in turn well matched to each individual client or prospect with which they are dealing.

Sometimes what needs to be done is counter-intuitive, in the way that faced with a complaint many people find it almost impossible to avoid making it clear that whatever happened was *not my fault* even though that is the last thing anyone wants to hear. The overall prevailing standard of property salesmanship is by no means all good, and there is much that is bad or at least unthinking and poorly focused on clients. Many people muddle through thinking that all that is necessary is a personable approach — *if people like me they will buy from me* — they say. They make sales (provided what they sell is good) but they will never sell as much as they could.

What does all this mean? *It means that those who tackle this area and get it right have a considerable opportunity to maximise sales results and thus positively influence the growth and profitability of the business in which they work.*

Selling is the most personal area of marketing. It is what *you* (or your colleagues) do that can guarantee success, and is heavily influenced by *what* you say and *how* you say it. The intention of this book is to provide guidelines and approaches that will enable you to sharpen your sales skills and maximise the results they produce. Nothing here is intellectually taxing. Good selling, to a large extent, is common sense. However, it is complex. In a client meeting that lasts even half an hour (and some last much longer), there is a great deal happening and many things to remember. Nevertheless, what needs to be done is well within the competence of most property professionals.

Furthermore, the same solution and approach is not right for every client, much less for every occasion. Rather an appropriate way forward must be found literally day-by-day, client-by-client and meeting-by-meeting. Selling is dynamic and changing market situations demand a flexible approach. The best people do not operate by rote, they do not "script" their presentation and they are always conscious of the fine detail of what they do. Indeed, a specific and individual client focus is essential to everything in the sales process and is a theme of this book throughout its length (it is inherent in the definition of selling referred to later).

It is such an approach that this book examines. It shows you how to:

- View the process of buying and selling.
- Understand and utilise the psychology of human nature (relating to buyer and seller) that is involved — turning theory into practice if you like.
- Adopt the right attitude to what you do, both to increase the chances of getting agreement and foster the professional relationship that you aim to create.
- Deploy tried and tested approaches that give you the best chance of differentiating yourself and your organisation in a crowded market and successfully persuading your clients to buy, to buy again and to buy more.

No fancy gimmicks are necessary; the most important element here is you. You can make your selling truly effective just by the way you go about it.

How to use this book to maximise your personal selling results

There are two ways this book can help you:

- First, it can help you improve and fine-tune your own personal professional selling skills. This applies whether you are a full-time sales person or a property professional with sales among the tasks with which you must cope. It will help whether you are doing this day-to-day or have just a handful of deals to win in a year.
- Second, the messages it spells out may need to be relayed on to those within your organisation who also undertake any kind of selling role; in which case, if you manage those people you surely need to know yourself exactly how they should be operating.

The book is arranged to broadly follow the chronology of events: from preparing for a meeting and getting off to a good start, right through to gaining a commitment at the end, what is called closing, successfully. Thus, it *dissects the process* and in so doing it may take longer to go through a review of the process than it sometimes does to execute it in real life. So be it. At the end of the day, you will only be able to maximise the effectiveness of your selling by attention to every aspect of it. So, although each part of the book makes sense in its own right, there is a compounding effect here: stage-by-stage the approaches gain in their power as they knit together to help you produce a seamless and natural conversation to which buyers find they respond positively. Thus, the whole is more useful than the parts individually, and you will get the most from the book by bearing this in mind as you go.

There are individual ideas here; things designed to make the description within your sales presentation more powerful for instance. You will also progressively find that the best way to orchestrate your overall approach and manage the complete communication emerges too.

After you have read the book, and perhaps annotated it a bit or made some notes about where ideas seem to suit you best, you can begin to incorporate ideas into what you do. I recommend that you do not try to revamp your entire approach, certainly not all at once. Rather, if there are ideas you decide to incorporate into your approach, try fine-tuning different aspects of what you do progressively. This keeps the process manageable, and prevents you from trying to concentrate on too much simultaneously, thus making it difficult to keep all the balls in the air at once.

With these points in mind, and always with an eye on competitive market conditions, let the review begin.

The Challenge of Competitive Markets

Winning business was never easy. Today, in competitive and dynamic markets, it can be downright difficult.

Clients are demanding, fickle and, above all, professional. They know what they want and they do not want anything other than a professional approach from the sales people with whom they deal; no where is this more true than when dealing with people who are also effectively the production resource and will be involved in work that is done after agreement is reached. Competitors cannot be relied on to miss a trick and everything done to develop business must be well chosen to do the job that the market and circumstances demand.

We review a variety of aspects of the specific task of selling all designed to help put you in a position where you can maximise the chances of success.

The nature of selling

There is a danger that selling is undertaken without sufficient care. It can seem easy: if you know what you provide, and it is good, surely all you have to do is tell people about it? Not so, as we will see. This danger is a real one too, but only if you take the wrong view of the sales process. Selling is not something you can regard as "doing to people". This makes the process seem inappropriately one-way, when it should be a dialogue.

The best definition I know of selling is that it is *"helping people to buy"*.

This may seem simple, but it characterises the process well. Prospects want to go through a process of decision-making, indeed they will do so whatever you may do. So, the core of what makes the basis for sales technique is a two-way process and both elements start on the client's side of the relationship. Always, we must consider the way in which people buy. Those buying products and services investigate options and weigh up the pros and cons of any given case (and often, of course, they are intentionally checking out several competing options alongside each other).

How do they do this? They go through a particular sequence of thinking. One way of looking at this, defined by psychologists way back, is paraphrased in seven points. They say to themselves:

1. I am important and want to be respected.
2. Consider my needs.
3. Will your ideas help me?
4. What are the facts?
5. What are the snags?
6. What shall I do?
7. I approve/disapprove.

Each step in the process must be taken before the buyer will willingly move on to the next one. Some decisions can be taken at once while others require a pause between each stage. The core of this process is that the buyer is weighing up the pros and cons of making a decision. The buyer wants to be able to make an appropriately informed decision; they put different points on one side of a metaphorical balance or the other. Nothing is perfect, so what wins is best thought of as what has the most positive balance. Thus, in competitive situations, a case can be won, or lost, on the basis of just one or two small points swinging the balance one way or another.

The process of making buying decisions always follows this seven-stage process. But execution of the process can be complex and reflects the nature of the client's business; the size of their organisation; the people and functions involved; their needs, and the degree of influence they have on buying decisions — and what they are buying. For example, an organisation considering which architect to commission for the job of designing and building a new warehouse is likely to go through a more complex process than that of an individual deciding where to have their car serviced. Essentially, the higher the price involved the greater the consideration that goes into the deliberations. Selling is best viewed from this perspective. As has been said, it is not something that you do *to* people — it is the mirror image of the buying process — something that is inherently two-way. This is as important for selling more to existing and past clients as it is to winning new business.

Selling is a process of needs satisfaction and research shows two facts that are extremely valuable to sellers. First, that sales meetings are much more successful when the client's needs are clearly identified. Second, as a result they are less successful when their needs are only implied. Asking is thus as important as telling.

Nothing is successfully sold unless a client willingly buys. Offering satisfied needs as reasons for buying — more of this later — encourages this but to follow the buying mind's seven-step process is vital whatever aspect of property you are involved in. There is a need to relate closely what is done in selling to the client's point of view; this can be done only if it is thought through carefully. Therefore, your sales approach must be planned.

In selling you are in the business of playing a part in clients' decision-making processes, assisting them to make decisions — the right ones — rather than pressurising them into it. The seller must be, in part, an advisor. Being an advisor simply does not fit with a high-pressure approach. This means that the typical fear of the professional that too much of a hard sell approach will switch people off, may be true, but it is not a real danger, because that is not what needs to be done to sell effectively.

If the right approach is adopted, making accepted deals more likely to be confirmed, then understanding and using the psychology of buying as a foundation to make your selling successful is a prime factor in making it work — successful selling is *helping people to buy*.

With that in mind, we turn to the complete process involved in the personal sales task.

The structure of the sales task

The actual task facing sales people can be described across a number of stages:

- *Prospect identification*: In some businesses, selling is directed at a well-known group (as with books to bookshops). In some sectors, repeat business with existing clients must be sold. Others need a constant supply of new prospects; for instance, contrast a surveyor and an estate agent. Some prospects identify themselves. They are recommended to you or respond to some aspect of your firm's promotional activity perhaps. In most aspects of property, an active approach is necessary too. It is necessary to decide whom to see (and who not to) and to put some priorities to prospects. This may need following up by promotional or sales action: using a variety of techniques from direct mail to networking techniques.

- *Planning*: With prospects in mind, and a meeting in prospect, some preparation is necessary. Success is not so likely by just "winging it" or dependence on technical wizardry; an approach must be tailored to achieve specific aims and matched to each particular prospect dealt with.
- *Handling the sales meeting*: Selling needs approaching systematically: a meeting needs some structure and must be designed to take an amount of time acceptable to the prospect. The plan is like a route map: as important to assist when it is not possible to follow the planned route, as it is when we can. The course of a meeting cannot be dictated, it must follow the input of the prospect to some degree even though you will want to keep it as much as possible on your track.

In thinking through the best approach, it helps to consider the logical stages of a meeting:

- *Opening*: The first moments, making a good first impression, identifying needs and setting the scene for the way you want to describe your offering.
- *Presentation*: Presenting your case, and making it understandable, attractive and credible to ensure it can act persuasively. How this is done, the power and precision of your description and more are vital to success. So too is recognising what the case needs to focus on. Some factors are of course technical, but other factors may seem less central to any technical brief. For example, I once saw a residents' association committee interview potential agents to manage the common land of a development, and the likelihood of good and regular communications was a factor rated highly, yet was barely mentioned by one of the potential agents.
- *Handling objections*: Any pitch is likely to give rise to some objections (which may only be clarifying questions) and this stage too must be handled smoothly.

- *Gaining a commitment ("closing")*: Closing does not cause people to buy, but it is usually necessary to take the initiative and ask for the business, converting the interest you have generated into actual orders.

The job here is multifaceted. The overall progress of the meeting must be controlled and managed and, at the same time, individual sales techniques must be deployed as appropriate and how things are done adjusted in the light of how the meeting is going. The key details of all this must comprise the plan (we return to the details in chapter 2).

- *Follow up*: A simple description of a far-reaching activity. If the prospect agrees, then the contact needs maintaining. If they hesitate, persistent chasing needs to take place, and yet be made acceptable. Beyond that, those that become regular accounts need managing and strategies developing to secure, develop and build future business.

The sales task is far from routine (despite much about its image). It needs a careful, systematic and creative approach demanding considerably more precision in the way it is done than the application of the traditional "gift of the gab". At base the key to it all is seeing things from the point of view of the client — the classic sales empathy — and using that to fine-tune approaches to ensure both persuasiveness and an approach that is acceptable, and appeals, to clients.

The right frame of mind

Make no mistake, the way you think about the process is the first thing that conditions how well it goes and what results you obtain. It is your attitude that decides how you will go about the detail of the job, and that in turn will influence how your clients see you and whether they are willing to do business with you. You may, after all, often be the only one present with the client on the day. So, in part to illustrate the approaches that the market demands, consider three key approaches you can take to what you do and how you do it, all of which can influence sales results positively and help to create the appropriate relationship. They are:

1. *Adopt the right overall approach*

Let us start with an overall point and one of the considerable significance. Selling must be regarded in the right way. It is dynamic, that is, it operates against a background of change. Markets, competition, and the economy are all subject to change; so are, most important of all, the clients. They are ever more demanding, ever more fickle, quick to take advantage of competitive pressures and wanting, understandably enough, value for money and service that meets their definition of both. Their attitudes may change; they are all individuals and expect to be dealt with in a way that recognises just that.

What works best in selling is, as a result, not any one set approach. Selling must deploy appropriate approaches from all the available techniques and do so client-by-client, meeting-by-meeting and day-by-day. The most successful people are those who recognise this fact. They seek to consciously fine-tune what they do, they never get stuck in a rut but always approach what they do intelligently and judge exactly how to proceed in the light of all the circumstances.

This fact alone can be crucial. Because elements of the sales task are necessarily repetitive, it is easy to get things done on "automatic pilot" and original and creative thinking about what is going on becomes less. As an example, one professional firm I worked with had a standard body of information about the firm (most often used in presentations and linked to, as I remember, 36 slides). Any mention of *something about the firm* and they automatically launched into this in identical fashion. It was certainly thorough, but too long and much of it was of no immediate relevance. Yet this had come about almost subconsciously and was easy to change when attention was focused on it.

Selling rarely has very much to do with good luck. Those selling can however, to an extent, make their own luck; certainly they can and will do better if they see the process of working at it as a continuous one. This affects all the other points mentioned in this book, indeed they are intended as prompts to just the kind of thinking described here. In other words, the person likely to be of most help to you in making your selling more effective is yourself.

2. *Be self-motivated*

Every book, certainly every American book, about selling discusses the need for a positive mental attitude. No doubt this can help selling, but you cannot pick positive mental attitudes off the trees or buy them in packs of six in the local supermarket. However, there are certain factors that do assist self-motivation in a practical sense. The wise person uses these to boost their thinking and assist their performance. Here we consider two areas that work in this way: *confidence and persistence*.

First, let us consider *confidence*. This is a question of belief, and while it is perhaps impossible to show how to create this within yourself, certainly in a short paragraph, there is one overriding principle that helps. That is to use those tangible factors on which confidence rests. For example, if you have done your homework — you are prepared — this boosts confidence, giving you things you can be sure of that otherwise might be imponderables. Similarly, knowing your "product knowledge" well, having clear objectives and sales aids that are tried, tested and ready all boost confidence. Bear this in mind as you read through this text, and see how many of the topics reviewed can help confidence in this way.

Second, consider *persistence*, a topic to which we return in a number of ways in the following pages. If you do more, rather than less, if you do more than others, then you know you are that much more likely to hit revenue targets. Productivity applies to selling just as much as to other areas of business.

Develop the habit of reviewing everything you do, answering one basic question: what can you do to operate more effectively? And you might be surprised how much better you feel about your abilities.

3. Resolve to constantly fine-tune your approaches

There is an old saying that you can have five years' experience or just one year's experience repeated five times over. This is simple yet vital. Experience needs to be taken and, at best, its accumulation accelerated. This concept is virtually universally accepted with regard to the technicalities of many jobs, indeed in those regarding themselves as professions with a capital "P" there is often a Continuing Professional Development (CPD) scheme of some sort to focus minds and ensure people keep up to date. So too in selling: see every client meeting you have as an opportunity to learn something that will help you make future calls work better, operating on the principle that even the best performance can be improved.

Probably more than anything else in marketing, sales activity prompts the best and most immediately useful feedback. Constantly ask questions of yourself. Why did someone say that? Why did they voice that objection? Did they misunderstand something? Did they agree? If you can develop the habit of spending a moment replaying most of your conversations in your mind after you have finished them, then you can use this analysis to gradually evolve new approaches for the future. Fine-tune the way you work and avoid getting into a rut, repeating endlessly the same phrases as if they were as relevant to all the different people you see, and what you do is more likely to remain fresh and well directed at each and every client.

So, another key to success is to use your personality and your knowledge to strengthen your sales approach — and use every client encounter to help make the next one more effective.

Part 2

A Foundation for Success

"I've never bought anything from ... people who didn't know the product and yet I have bought things I didn't know I needed from people who did."

Mark H McCormack

Planning and Preparation

Most things in life that are worth doing require some effort before they return any reward. It was the hair stylist Vidal Sassoon who is credited with saying: *"The only place where success comes before work is in the dictionary"*; he was correct. So do not pass over this chapter, believing that success or improvement will come more easily from the technique areas that follow it. They can doubtless help also, and are, perhaps, inherently more interesting, but preparation is vital. It is, in fact, one of the key factors that can help you differentiate yourself from competitors and ensure a good reception from those with whom you seek to do business. A number of points here investigate the main elements involved.

Do your homework

Because the thought of planning can be daunting, it may be skimped, however, you do this at your peril. There is an old story, which I have heard attributed to a dozen different professional golfers, of them saying something like: *"It's a funny thing, but it seems the more I practice the luckier I am on the day of the match"*. So it is with selling. Successful people make it look easy but, if they are good, then in all likelihood they have done their homework. Good luck is not to be relied on (although some say that it is the reason your competitors are successful!).

So, *always* prepare; doing so is taking the first step to giving themselves a real edge on competition. Make it a habit.

Sometimes preparation constitutes just a few minutes of thinking matters through before you go into a meeting. Sometimes this thinking takes place in the car outside the client's office where a few moments reviewing their file can pay dividends. Sometimes it may mean sitting round the table with a couple of colleagues debating the best approach to take with a key prospect. It takes time, some aspects of it may seem a chore, but it should always happen. A well-prepared sales situation should conceal fewer unforeseen pitfalls, and allow greater certainty of success. The person who resolves to regularly spend time on preparation is making a wise decision. The next sections explore particular ways of doing this.

Set clear objectives

There is a saying that: if you do not know where you are going, any path will do. Every meeting with a prospect or client needs clear objectives. If you do not have a clear idea of what you are trying to achieve it is difficult to set in train action to achieve it. To say the objective is to win business is too simplistic. What business exactly, by when, in what quantity, and how? Many objectives may be valid. You may want simply to find out information (to allow a next stage to take place); you may want to get agreement to make specific proposals, to quote, to run a trial, a survey or a demonstration; you may want to engineer an introduction to someone else — the real decision maker. And such objectives link together. A successful demonstration of some sort may lead to the opportunity to survey detailed requirements and subsequently quote on them, or report back in a formal presentation.

So clear objectives are important and they must be, as the well-known mnemonic puts it, SMART. That is:

- *Specific* — setting out clearly what you intend.
- *Measurable* — getting agreement to something specific that can be measured, clients give it or not, a more vague objective — "to increase awareness" — may be difficult to observe and measure.
- *Achievable* — can we reasonably do it? For example, it may sound agreeable for a surveyor to say that they want to take over responsibility for a whole property portfolio at a first meeting, but is there any chance it can really be done? If a trial order is the only real opportunity, then going for that makes a better objective.

- *Realistic* — here we must ask should we go for it. Sometimes we do not want the business. Maybe too large an order cannot be coped with (at a busy time, perhaps) and complaints will surely follow. Or perhaps there could be a clash in some businesses in having two major competitors as clients (they may both suspect secrets could be, unwittingly, betrayed); any conflict of interest is usually best avoided.
- *Timed* — this specifies when you intend something will be achieved. At the first meeting, the second, in six weeks, or a year on?

Some people talk of what they call "courtesy calls" with existing or past clients. There should be no such thing. There should always be a real reason — an objective — for the call, and while this is, in part introspective, concerned with what we want, you should also always think of *what is in it for the client*. If that is posed as a question and cannot be easily and convincingly answered, then you may need to reconsider the objective.

Give your clients a reason to find your contacts useful and it can be the first step towards successfully obtaining business.

Anticipate objections

You will know from experience that objections are not just possible, they are likely — indeed many say that receiving none is a sign of a total lack of interest. As your experience grows, few objections should come as a complete surprise to you. You come to know the sort of thing that gets raised. Furthermore, you learn the things different types of client raise — the one who is obsessed with every last tiny technical detail, the one who quibbles over your promises about timing.

To some extent you can, as you prepare, anticipate what a particular client may ask; and be ready to deal with it effectively. Of course, sometimes something will come out of the blue, and always the objection may be put in a different way from how it has occurred in the past. Preparing for them does not mean you can stop thinking during the meeting or that you have to have a "pat" answer ready, but it will make dealing with them more certain and make it less likely that they will unbalance the case you present so that the client rejects it. Some you may be able to prevent arising at all by thinking ahead. Prevention may be used as effectively as cure in this area.

Arrange suitable sales aids

This is an area of preparation easily overlooked. There is a parallel here with the executive whose desk is habitually untidy but who always, so they say, knows where to find everything. Really? Most people need to use sales aids of some sort. These may be anything from a graph, which illustrates and explains cost effectiveness, to a sample, an illustration, a chart, brochure or a complete demonstration — how many people would buy, say, a car without a test drive? These are used not simply because it seems like a good idea, but because the client demands it or experience has shown it improves the ability to explain or demonstrate. For example, an estate agent can demonstrate how property details will be prepared by showing ones for similar properties (a draft too may be regarded as still demonstrating how it *might* be). If aids are to be used they must be available, accessible and in pristine condition.

For research purposes, I once accompanied an architect on a client visit. He used sales aids with the bulk of the exhibits consisting of plans and details of past work. Being professionally prepared and appropriately selected, they were effective in enhancing the case he made to clients. In this particular meeting, I remember he was well into the meeting and all was going well, he mentioned the first exhibit and reached into his briefcase to get it out and show the client. Three or four minutes later he was still looking; we later found the folder he wanted on the back seat of his car. The way this diluted his credibility was marked, the client said "never mind" but his face said that he found it unforgivably inefficient; and no business was subsequently forthcoming.

The moral here is simple. Think about what you are going to need for every meeting and make sure you have everything you need organised, that it is in the right order for the particular meeting and that it is in a condition that will impress the client. Nothing short of 100% organisation in this respect is permissible if you want to avoid any dilution of your effectiveness.

Two heads can be better than one

By its nature, the job of winning business can be a solitary one. But this does not mean that you always have to do everything by yourself. There is merit in being self-sufficient, but one must not make a fetish of it. Selling is, or should be, a creative process.

It demands ideas and the consideration of various options in terms of action, and bouncing the idea off someone else may be a quicker, easier way to proceed and may produce a better solution than solitary rumination. The informal networks that exist around the firm may help here. If not, organising such a sounding board, seeking out a colleague with whom you can discuss things, perhaps on a reciprocal basis, can be helpful. So too, in larger firms, may be liaisons with senior managers.

Know your business

You have to be up to date on the situation, technicalities, and developments — gossip even — of your chosen area of business. Anything less destroys confidence in you being an expert in your field, an image that most professionals are at pains to cultivate. Again, keeping up to date is something that may take time. You have to read the trade and technical press and any appropriate literature in your field regularly, and you have to talk to the right people. Your company should help. If there are things you feel you should see (a journal your clients quote to you, perhaps) ask for them. Take whatever steps are necessary, but make sure you are always seen as being on the ball in this way. Clients buy most readily from people in whom they have confidence, and being one who manifestly knows their own business sends out useful signals.

Know your client's business

This goes with the point above and is, if anything, even more important. You need to understand the situation within which your clients work. Not just the technicalities, clearly if you work in a technical field you need to understand something of the technicalities, but also the whole scene: the hopes and fears, the way they think. Is their business growing or under pressure, have they had staff reductions, what is their cash flow like, how important is your product or service to their business and why?

There are many questions to ask yourself, and being sensitive to their situation in this way will show. Some things in this area come from observation and experience, some things about large organisations (if such are among your clients) are public and in the business press. But you can take more specific action too. For instance, many companies not only issue internal newsletters or magazines to their staff, but also they will send them on request to other interested parties or they can be picked up in their reception area. If so, make arrangements to see them. Reception areas are often a ready source of information about your clients, what you can see, pick up or overhear may be of real use. A friendly receptionist may also be a useful source of information.

Not only will a sound basis of knowledge be useful to you in selling, but it being observed that you take a real interest in your clients will be useful too. Your clients no doubt think that their organisations are the centre of the universe, and like people with whom they do business to express a real interest in it.

Know your product

This is vital. This book was typed on a laptop computer. It is a wonderful machine, it has changed my life and I could now not live without it. But ... finding someone who could explain it to me, answer my questions and reassure me that I was making the right decision to buy this particular one was a nightmare. Not only were people selling it unable to explain clearly, but they simply did not know the answers to what I regarded as basic points. What is more, I think this is a common complaint. On another occasion, I remember sitting though a 30-minute presentation about a proposed pension scheme to the board of a company. At the end the person making it asked whether there were any questions. To general agreement, the managing director announced, *"I don't think I understood any of that"*.

I repeat: exemplary product knowledge is vital. You need to know your product or service inside out. You need to know what it will do, why it does it and how. You need to be able to answer any question that potential clients want answered and be able to do so promptly and efficiently and often doing so succinctly is also important. Putting yourself in a position like this is vital; you are always going to be vulnerable until you have the relevant information — all of it — at your fingertips. So read the brochures, fact sheets and manuals and ask, ask, ask until you are satisfied with your ability in this area.

Then go on doing it to keep up to date.

Note: A form or checklist may be useful as you pull together your thoughts about any particular prospect or client. Completing such thinking before every meeting may be a useful discipline and need not take too long; certainly a few moments' thought must always precede a meeting of any sort with a client. Key topics to review include:

- Your call objectives.
- Key points of opening.
- Key points of the main presentation you will make.
- Objections it may be necessary to handle (and answers).
- Action/decisions that you intend to prompt from the client.
- Support items needed (eg visual aids, handouts, equipment, samples).

Make a plan, base it on sound information and sensible thinking and every client meeting will be a little easier to conduct and more likely to succeed.

Everything to do with preparation is important. Thorough preparation leads to good selling, and it is all too easy to come out of a meeting kicking yourself and wishing you had spent a moment longer on something beforehand so that it could have been better done. It may be obvious, but *ready, aim, fire!* really is the best order in which to proceed.

Focusing to Create the Best Potential

Apart from the quality of the face-to-face selling techniques to be reviewed later (which are certainly an area of major influence), there are only three key matters that influence the process of winning business. They are:

- *Who you see* — which particular prospects and clients you spend time with.
- *How many you see* — success is also a matter of productivity. In general terms, if you see more people then, all things being equal, you will sell more.
- *How often you see them* — the question of frequency of contact with people needing regular visits is vital (too little and there is no continuity or relationship developed, too much and overcalling reduces productivity and the number of new people you can see).

Clearly this needs interpreting differently in different parts of the property world, with, say, an estate agent seeing a higher number of people than an architect. Before you even consider which people you will see, you have to be able to take action that will result in a meeting; here we look at a number of points ahead of dealing with making initial contact in the next chapter. If most enquiries come to you, some of this may not be relevant, but even then it may be that not all the enquiries are from good prospects.

Seeing the right people

Two comments are relevant under this heading.

- First, that in some businesses the potential market is way beyond what the individual can contact. For example, an architect might aim to do anything to assist house owners, and face a market that is huge as a result.
- Second, which people do you attempt to see? The largest companies? The nearest? Those ones in a particular industry? And what kind of person do you see? Who uses your product or service, who has the budget, who makes the purchase decision? This might be the managing director of some organisations and a particular manager in another. Of course, they will not all need it and, even if they do, that need may already have been satisfied — perhaps your main competitor is already in touch with them. Superficially, they may all seem like prospects. Remember: not all acorns grow into giant oak trees — most are eaten by the pigs. Even those that register an enquiry are not equal prospects either.

So you must set priorities. Allowing your time to be wasted on those who exhibit no real potential, the "no-hopers", perhaps because they are in some way easy to access, will never do as well as those who accept that priorities must be set and then do so systematically. So the architect above may need to concentrate on people wanting home extensions, in a particular kind of house and geographic area and use more besides to focus what they do.

Trust your own experience, and never ignore past evidence. Ask yourself who has purchased in the past, and why. Think through the logic of contacting one person rather than others and concentrate your activities and your efforts, for example, on those which analysis shows are the best prospects. If you work in smaller defined areas, such as one county, this problem may hardly exist, as the potential clients are comparatively few in number and identifying them with a view to establishing contact with them all is not so hard. The incidence of new ones that need assessing in terms of potential is less. For other people it is key, and their success is in direct proportion to the time and sensible thought put into deciding who to see and who not to see; at least not yet. Who you decide to see is perhaps the first decision that influences whether business is likely to result; so choose carefully.

Who is the buyer?

At first sight, this may seem a stupid question. At one level you need to identify the person who buys: QED. However, *the* buyer is often, particularly in some aspects of the property world, more than one person, or at least more than one person plays a part in the buying process. It is useful to categorise the different roles that may be involved. An example illustrates the principle. Say a new office is to be sought or built.

- *The users*: any member of staff may have opinions about it, and some may be involved in the decision; a head of department say.
- *Advisors*: these people act as advisors to someone who will make the decision, here, perhaps, the administration director is charged with collecting opinions, defining a brief and advising someone higher up. The accountant too may be an advisor, at least on cost, contracts and financing.

If the company has a purchasing department, someone there may be the buyer who is actually influenced by all those others already mentioned and who has, in addition, a measure of authority, large or small, themselves.

- *Decision makers*: when the final recommendation, or short list, is in, it may be the managing director who is the decision maker; equally, it may be others throughout the hierarchy of the organisation. Having said all that, the person who rings up in the first instance investigating the possibility of obtaining your help may be someone quite different, such as the accountant's secretary.

You must never assume that whoever initiates contact, or responds to your overtures to see them is, by definition, the ultimate decision maker. You need to know what role they play, who else is involved and how the ultimate decision will be made. This may only emerge progressively as the contact is progressed, and the information about how it all works may need to be actively unearthed by active, but careful, questioning.

To add a small complication, there is another category that is worth attention and which plays a part in all this. They are usually called the *gatekeepers* and are investigated below.

The role of the gatekeeper

The internal role of the gatekeeper is often all too clear. It is to prevent people with something to sell (and others) wasting the time of those further up the organisation. However, they do realise that some such people are valuable, and may be persuaded to see their role as making a sensible assessment rather than fending off every caller. One thing is certain. They do not like to be treated as insignificant or dealt with without respect. Treat them carefully, ask their help, imply you can help them and their bosses and they can become an asset to your winning business.

Specifically, gatekeepers are those who can provide access to others who then play a more significant role in the buying process. If a manager is the decision maker, then his secretary is likely to be a gatekeeper. She may not be the only one, switchboard operators and receptionists often have a gatekeeping role. Such people may be comparatively junior in the hierarchy of the buying organisation, but they can still wield considerable power as far as a sales person is concerned. You must recognise who the gatekeepers are and then always treat them with respect. Develop a relationship, and remember to say thank you when appropriate. Show them they are important to you, but never patronise them. Some have sharp teeth as it were and will savage anyone who tries to use them in an obvious way. They are important, so saying so and dealing with them in this way can surely be natural.

Remember that they will not all be junior, some people have this role although they are themselves senior. Within the property world, an architect, for instance, may or may not allow access to their principal who may be the supremo on some major construction or development project. In turn, the architect's secretary or assistant will protect access to them. So there may be tiers of gatekeepers. A final point: if they are not people you meet in the automatic course of your dealings with clients, then you may need to seek them out.

However you come across them, gatekeepers make good friends, but as enemies are no good at all for your chances of selling.

Never assume you know the decision maker. Inquire, investigate and direct your attentions accurately.

Note: the next chapter is about prospecting — making "cold" approaches to those you do not know. If you are sure that your business does not necessitate your undertaking prospecting activities — ever — then feel free to skip chapter 4.

Finding the Best Prospects

The balance of managing existing clients and yet constantly finding sufficient new ones to grow and develop the business can be crucial. Sometimes it is aspects of marketing activity that play the greatest role here, with a steady flow of enquiries prompted by elements of the marketing mix producing the bulk of the required new contacts. For most, some part of the required number must come from more individual and personal activity; and sometimes this demands a significant volume of such activity.

Yet, when this is so, it is all too often something that is found difficult, distasteful and neglected; one feels there is a clear link here between these factors, and that it is not simply that "cold calling" is incompatible with creating a professional image and relationship. It is precisely because prospecting is inclined to be difficult to fit in among other work priorities, and do justice to, that it must be approached systematically. In this chapter, we review the approaches and methodology that can make it effective when it is appropriate, which is not the case for the whole property sector.

Make prospecting a regular activity

There can be hardly anyone born who does not find "cold calling" less attractive than calling on existing clients. This is not surprising. It is unlikely to be easy, the strike rate is likely to be lower and, by definition, the rejection rate will be higher. Yet many businesses need the lifeblood of a constant supply of new prospects at least to some extent. If you need a regular supply of potential new clients, then you must recognise that the activity to produce them must itself be carried out regularly. It is a common fault of many sales people that they neglect or put off action in this area, allowing an insufficient number of prospects to become a major problem.

If new contacts are the lifeblood of your business, make your first rule of prospecting: do it, and do it systematically and regularly.

Set time aside every week, month or whatever, give yourself some targets and link prospecting to regular activities; do not let other, short-term pressures give you the excuse to neglect it. Do it regularly and the returns you get from it will help you achieve the results you want.

Create prospecting methods that work for you

Prospecting is a state of mind. It is a habit and, as such, helped by cultivating a range of ways of doing it that can themselves become habits. These then can become a regular source of new leads and you do not have to think of a fresh way of producing every new contact you need. There are many ways of doing this and you need to find methods that suit you and your business. The following examples may themselves be useful and may also be illustrative of how a range of different techniques can be developed. Make a point of trying to develop more or of adapting these, changing them to suit your own use.

Here are 10 specific ways as examples of how to unearth new contacts:

(1) Endless chain

This is simply, as the name suggests, using one prospect to lead to another. A first may come, let us say, as an enquiry. Once you know who they are, what they might be interested in, why they came to you — in other words, as you begin to find out about them, you can ask who else they can direct you to.

This may be in two ways:

- *Asking*: "do you know anyone else who might be interested ...?"
- *Analysing*: "if this developer is interested, which others can I talk to?"

(2) Centres of influence

These are people or organisations through whom you may make contact with numbers of prospects on a regular basis, because they have the power to introduce or recommend. They may include trade and professional bodies, chambers of commerce, associations, banks and others, including professional bodies (although beware of spending too much time mixing with competitors rather than potential clients). It is worth thinking through which may be useful in your business, listing them and systematically keeping in touch to ensure they know of you, they know what you do, and are reminded of this and kept up to date. (Share the task of keeping in touch with colleagues, with each taking responsibility for a number of such contacts. I have seen numerous examples of firms analysing and reviewing the list of possible bodies, reallocating them among colleagues and seeing immediate benefit from so doing.) Any such networking, which can lead to new clients, is likely to be both worthwhile and cost effective if contact is maintained systematically.

(3) Personal observation

This should never be underestimated. If you develop the habit of being observant, then a regular supply of new prospects can follow. First, consider things in print. You need to review regularly any journals, newspapers or publications relevant to your business. Trade or industry journals are a good example. So are in-house newsletters if you have major companies as clients who produce them, and they will often put you on the list — providing you ask. News of companies, developments, staff changes, relocation and more can all provide information to lead you to a new prospect, as can websites.

Second, keep your eyes open and check anything that might help you. Ask yourself: who has moved into the new office block on the corner, or into the offices next door to someone you already know? Again, such observation (and perhaps a little associated research) can lead to new names and thus new prospects.

(4) Chance contacts

This is closely related to personal observation, but worth a separate mention. I have twice obtained work following a conversation with someone sitting next to me on an aeroplane, when idle chatter identified common business interests. I once even obtained work from someone whose office I wandered into, lost, to seek directions in the bowels of an office block. Beware, of course, of taking this too far, but keep an eye open for such opportunities, particularly in places where people of similar interests meet — a trade association meeting, perhaps.

(5) "Cold canvass"

Simply knocking on doors is probably not to be recommended to anyone but the least faint-hearted. However, one variant may well be useful. In places where different businesses exist close by, such as on an industrial estate or in an office block, it may be worthwhile knocking on some doors near to an existing visit; not to try to sell them something, but to discover names. Ask the receptionist for names of those in key positions. Again, even a few names may be useful and they will be geographically convenient too, which aids productivity if you subsequently need to visit them regularly.

(6) Lists

Not so much the large ones such as *Yellow Pages*, but the small specialist ones. Association membership lists, interest groups, professional bodies; whatever ties in with your business area. This can yield names for small mailings, and can be made manageable by being reviewed progressively with mailings following at so many per week. Some research on what lists exist is often worthwhile.

(7) Past clients/contacts

If you are systematic there should be few of these. Despite that, realistically there will likely be some. People have good reasons sometimes for stopping doing business with you, some that have nothing to do with you; someone leaves the company, a budget is cut, expenditure is delayed — there are many reasons. If so, always check when things may change again, note it in the diary, however far ahead, and remember to get in touch again and keep in touch as appropriate during any enforced gap. If you have *not* been very systematic in the past, it may well be worth a comprehensive research of the "archives". I know one firm that labels certain files and systems involved in this sort of process as LYBUNT (Last Year But Unfortunately Not This) to make a point about contacts dying of neglect.

Note: A client for one product in your range, but apparently not for another, may be persuaded to buy both. Thus a consultant retained for planning advice, might also persuade the client to extend the brief and involve them in design work too.

(8) Suppliers

Anyone you do business with might be persuaded to do business with you if your product is something they buy. You know them. They know you. They doubtless want to retain your business, so they are unlikely to reject a suggestion to talk out of hand.

Furthermore, you will no doubt have a good record of such people in your accounts department, and need to do little more than check through the invoices they send you to identify them.

(9) Extra curricular activities

Business and pleasure do not always mix, but sometimes they do. A good number of business deals really are struck on the golf course just as legend would have it (although these are perhaps usually deals between people who already know one another). It may be worth reviewing what you do, where you go, what clubs or associations you belong to, and seeing whether you can get more from them in a business sense. This is worth a thought but must definitely be the subject of care, after all the committee may not approve (although if you were on the committee maybe you would make more contacts). This, and other activities mentioned come under the general heading of networking. This is not a vague term and its usefulness can be maximised if it is used systematically. It may be worthwhile to investigate networking, and indeed its wider applications, separately then you can do no better than read networking guru Frances Kay's forthcoming book on communication in the property world and also published by EG Books.

(10) Directories

There are so many directories published that, certainly in the UK, there is a directory of directories. This implies there could well be one or

paid for having many more, albeit smaller ones, and it is a wise man who never trusts anything crucial to memory. If you have the details of all that your company offers and maybe of a significant number of clients and prospects buzzing round in your head, it is simply unrealistic to believe you will retain every last detail. Write it down (advice I will not apologise for repeating more than once as we go through the book). You do not want to forget names you have found and action you have planned — *I'll ring you again towards the end of the month* you say, or in two or three months — and you have to be 100% certain of doing it. And not only for your own benefit; promises must be kept and it can be impressive when they are. So whether it is in a diary, notebook or an electronic organiser or computer system, note every name, every number and note also specific action — when you will telephone or visit and when, if necessary, you will do so again and again.

Making appointments

Of course, there are people you can see without an appointment, and types of selling where appointments are not the norm, although this is less usual in property than in some fields. However, there are good reasons to make them wherever possible and signs also that clients are increasingly reluctant to see people without the visit being prearranged. First, appointments being a high proportion of your meetings tend to make you more productive; you can manage your time better. Second, clients like to be dealt with this way and that may be reason enough.

Appointments can be made for a specific meeting. Other appointments are longer term, but can still be made, at least as a general commitment, well in advance. An agreed quarterly or even annual review meeting may be arranged; a telephone call nearer the time being used to confirm and set an exact time. Maybe I should agree with the publisher now while writing this to meet with them to hand over the manuscript, and see if there is anything more I can do for them!

Other kinds of appointment making are more difficult, such as cold calling or even following up a prospect's request for more information. A real initiative must be taken and it helps if such a call (they are almost always on the telephone) abides by certain rules:

- Open clearly and positively.
- Have a reason for calling that you can describe in client terms to show what is in it for them.

- Have a reason for setting a meeting (rather than some other action they could take) perhaps something they will see.
- Talk about the meeting as working with the client, do not sound as if you want to do something to them.
- Suggest alternative times, the first more specific than the second: *"How about 3.30 on Wednesday afternoon, or would sometime on Thursday or Friday suit you better?"* Offer times in pairs of alternatives.
- Do not give up if they cannot see you in the next week or so, an arrangement three weeks or three months, or even a year ahead, is still positive interest.

Finally, consider confirming in writing and check all appropriate details (do you have the address, is there parking available, and so on).

Do not base your approach on a lie

I once saw a company appraisal form on which managers were asked to mark their subordinates from 1 to 10 on a list of characteristics and performance factors. One of the entries called for a mark for honesty. This seemed to me to be nonsense. In business you are usually either honest or you are fired. But there is that convenient in between: the so-called white lie.

There may well be a place for these if life and relationships are to work, but there are some much-used phrases that are so transparent as be to the equivalent of putting up a large illuminated sign that says, *This is only a ploy*. Consider some examples that sales people say:

- *"I will be in your area on Thursday"* — rubbish, it only ever means they will be there if the prospect agrees to see them. And even if it were true it is not a good reason to offer a new prospect; why should they be concerned about your convenience?
- *"I will take only 10 minutes of your time"* — rubbish, it takes some people this long to get the formalities out of the way and get down to business. Clients just see this as a lie.
- *"I can only make this offer today"* (or to you) — this sounds as if you say it to everyone, every day.
- *"I was recommended to contact you"* — by whom? Too often this just means that the prospect's name is out of the directory.

It is all too reminiscent of the old buyer's response *"If I believed that, you would be able to sell me the Great Pyramid"*. You can no doubt think of more phrases and may, perhaps, even think of some you are inclined to use that are similar in texture. Clients are not fooled for a second by such phrases. They will just be seen as a sign of little or no preparation, having no clear objective and not treating them with respect. Avoid this sort of start to any conversation; it represents a style of selling wholly incompatible with creating professional relationships.

Now, with a good prospect in mind (or indeed an existing or past client), and a considered plan as to how to deal with them too, a sales meeting can take place. Part three reviews the details of how best to handle this — stage-by-stage, indeed moment-by-moment, including matters that may appear peripheral but which can be important.

Part 3

Conducting Effective Sales Meetings

"A salesman has to use his imagination, deliberately and consciously, to think up just what little things he can do to be helpful to each client. Every case calls for different tactics."

Alex F Osborn

First Impressions Last

It may be an old cliché, but you only get one chance to make a good first impression. Its truth makes it worth repeating. If you get off to a good start, everything else you will do thereafter during a sales meeting will be just a little easier. A good start affects the client and it affects your confidence positively. This does not just happen, it starts with preparation and then needs to be actively worked at to ensure you achieve the impact you want. And it is worth going for, especially for the professional who is having to bolt on selling skills to their already complex professional credentials; it makes a real difference, as the points here demonstrate.

First base

Everyone, if they are honest, knows the temptation of making snap judgments about people. We all tend to do it, and, what is more, such impressions tend to be both firm and yet time often proves them inaccurate. So it is with others and for us. Therefore, you should give no excuse for the wrong impression to be formed about you. Doing so links back to preparation. If you are well prepared then you should be more confident and better able to make a good start. This is not a question of gimmicks or an overdone approach, but of being business-like and aware of the need for everything to go well early on — having such an intention is the first step to achieving it.

Things such as:

- A greeting and polite recognition of initial conventions.
- Links to previous conversations.
- Stating a clear, client and benefit-orientated reason for the discussion.

all help. And even before this a display of appropriate manners, waiting to be asked to sit down for example, is also necessary. Of course, client relationships become more relaxed as you get to know a client, but such courtesies should always be borne in mind and have an effect on how a client will react early on.

Looking the part

It is common sense to look the part, and be smartly dressed. In this book, which the publisher assures me will be on sale in various parts of the world, I would not presume to lay down the law about dress. Suffice it to say that prevailing standards are best followed, so that a suit matters most in England, whereas only a shirt and tie will normally display the same degree of formality in, say, Singapore where it is too hot for jackets. It is always important to be clean and tidy. Again some businesses set their own style, with someone selling, say, at the more creative end of things dressing in a more avant-garde fashion — but if in doubt as to the conservatism of your client; it is perhaps better to be less fashionable and acceptable than vice versa.

This is an area for common sense; I remember conducting a presentation rehearsal for a firm of architects. It was a presentation to be made to a Town Council in the north-west of England. All the signs were that they would be a conservative group of people. One of the three people to speak at the meeting was, let us say, fashionably dressed. I asked him what he would look like on the day. His managing director instantly chipped in sternly, *"He'll look appropriate, won't you?"* Horses for courses; it only demands a moment's thought and some empathy for the client. This is also an area, incidentally, where women have to juggle a greater range of possibilities than men.

What you must certainly do is look efficient, and that is influenced by many things, all of which you need to think about in advance. You may look personally fine until you open your briefcase to display the inside looking like a rubbish dump. It does not even matter if you succeed in finding everything, untidiness will affect your image for the worse. This principle includes being suitably kitted out for the job in hand. For example, if you visit building sites or country properties you may need a pair of wellington boots in the back of your car, and similarly some property jobs may need overalls. There are some too who put their faith in "power dressing", believing that if you have the right tie, the best shoes and the correct accessories, then this makes all the difference to your image. There may be some truth in this, however, I heard of someone telephoned out of the blue by a prospect. *"One of your competitors has just been to see me and, as I noticed he parked a Porsche outside, I think I could do with another quote."* So do not overdo it.

Starting as you mean to go on

Getting off to a good start is not simply a question of impressions, there is a very business-like aspect to it, one that lasts throughout the meeting with the client. Consider: only one person at a time can truly direct a conversation, one leads and the other tends to follow. This does not mean there is no give and take, and it does not mean that one party is subservient, but one does lead and if you are wearing your selling hat there is merit in being the one that does so. Whether you successfully get hold of the meeting, and thus put yourself in the driving seat as it were, depends on how you act. Certainly a role that directs must be taken up in a way that is totally acceptable to the client.

Two points here help:

- Beware that a chatty start to the meeting, a part of the proceedings for which you may have no real plan, does not lead to the client chipping in with something that leads you in what is, for you, the wrong direction. Make no mistake, however, meetings do take a moment to start; we need to go through some ritual of getting started, we talk rather pointlessly of the weather, the traffic or where to park until someone says something: *"Right, let's get on, can you tell me ..."*. If the client makes this switch then it may be difficult to get back on track, and the initiative may have been lost. If you contribute a more relevant start, it gives you something you can deal with and move towards the business of the meeting.
- One technique that works well for the professional is to suggest an agenda for the meeting. This does not need to be stated as more than a helpful suggestion. It can be modified in discussion, but

once agreed it allows you to proceed along lines that suit you; indeed it provides an element of control throughout the meeting as you refer back to it (for instance saying, *Right, we agreed to take X next* ...) and move on to the next stage. The early part of any meeting is a key stage both for your confidence, you feel and thus operate better if you get off to a good start, and to the control and direction of the meeting.

Resolve always to sell from the driving seat, and take action to make it possible while ensuring it always appears only helpful; everything that follows is then easier.

The manner most likely to succeed

The overall manner deployed most likely to make selling successful can be characterised by the interrelation of two factors. These are projection and empathy:

- *Projection* encompasses everything about the way you come across: power, personality, weight, authority, and expertise. This is sometimes called "clout".
- *Empathy* is the ability to put you in someone else's place and see things from their point of view (more of this in chapter 6).

Both are important, but it is the way they are put to work together that creates the right impression. Too much of either holds dangers and the figure on p45 shows graphically four classic arrangements. This is not intended as an academic view of things but can provide a measure of how you are coming across, which, if you keep it in mind, can help you maintain a balance as you go along. Because anything that smacks too much of sales may be viewed with at least some suspicion, adopting the right manner, one that makes sense in terms of what clients want from your kind of organisation, makes very good sense.

It is possible to categorise four distinct types of approach on an axis of high and low projection and high and low empathy — the balance here is important. Both elements contribute to achieving the right manner; although as either can be overdone, some care is necessary. Keeping this balance in mind and actively working throughout any meeting to get the mix right will help you to be persuasive while being seen by clients as a reasonable person with whom to deal and with whom they can have a suitable professional relationship.

High projection

Type 1 High pressure	*Type 4* Ideal/persuasive

Low   **High**

Empathy   **Empathy**

Type 2 Take it or leave it	*Type 3* Weak

Low projection

Type 1: The "high pressure" sales person is over aggressive and insensitive. They feel they win the argument but, in fact, their projection, without empathy, becomes self-defeating and switches people off. The archetypal high-pressure sales person is the popular image of, say, a double-glazing sales person; surely not right for this sector.

Type 2: The "take it or leave it" sales person has little interest in the other person, nor their own ideas. A lack of commitment to the whole process tends to let it run into the sand. The archetypical take it or leave it person is characterised by the unhelpful shop assistant with whom most of us are all too familiar.

Type 3: The "weak" sales person is one who "means well". They have good sensitivity to the other person, come across as essentially nice, but take the side of the listener so that persuasion vanishes and they achieve little commitment. This is a type noticeable among professionals; beware.

Type 4: The "ideal" sales person is seen as having a creative understanding of the listener, being well-informed and producing both agreement and commitment to the satisfaction of both sides. Being seen to see the other person's point of view is, in itself, crucial.

Figure 5.1 Factors influencing the manner of sales approach

Blend being empathetic (you must not only *be* empathic, you must *be seen to be empathetic*) with a degree of confidence and assertiveness — aim to be the kind of person someone will *have confidence in buying from*.

Again, this further positions the professional approach that is necessary for success in the property world.

Use eye contact

In most cultures, avoiding another person's eye is regarded as shifty. Yet the first stages of a sales meeting are such that they do present some psychological difficulties. You wonder what the buyer thinks of you, you worry about how the meeting will go, you have a good deal to concentrate on to try to make sure it does go well; all may hinder an open approach. Yet if you can look the client in the eye and develop an easy manner to go with it, then you are much more likely to give the right impression.

Much of the impact eye contact has is to do with the amount of time eye contact is maintained. Less than one-third of the time can result in you being read as untrustworthy. More than one-third of the total time with eye contact tends to indicate interest in the other person, which will be just what a client expects from you, so ideally to build reasonable rapport you should be in eye contact 60/70% of the time. When eye contact drops below the level of the other person's face, a less formal atmosphere is created. And looking away completely, slow blinking or closing the eyes for longer periods than normal can be a clear indication of lack of interest or, worse, boredom.

A final point, gestures can direct eye contact. Pointing to something you are showing a client directs their eyes towards it, lifting the head and engaging eye contact again will change the emphasis of the meeting. Such points are part of what is called body language and, while this is not a science nor is it able to offer infallible signs, it can be useful and may be something worth investigating separately as it is beyond our brief here.

So you are off to a good start, you have your objectives in mind, you have succeeded in making your client feel that following your agenda is, for them, the best way to proceed. What next? You cannot — must not — do much else without knowing something about the client; that is each particular individual client (remember they are all different). It is to these differences that we turn to next.

Every Client is Different

6

Without clients, preferably satisfied clients coming back for more, your revenue will be nil. Clients are all unique, changes in the way professional services are sold, coupled with competitive markets in the property world, make them increasingly fickle, and they are usually demanding and may often seem difficult — although there is an old saying: *"No client is worse than no client"* — certainly they require some understanding. Understanding them does not just make your job easier, it is inherent to the whole process of ensuring a client relates to you in a manner that plays a part in prompting them to do business with you. Thus the points below focus on this key part of the sales process.

The need for understanding

Clients expect that people intent on doing business with them will understand them; really understand them; and they do this in two ways:

- They expect people to be well briefed about their industry, product, kind of business (or personal circumstances, if appropriate) — whatever is appropriate. Remember what was said about "homework" earlier. You should take active steps to make sure that your level of knowledge in this way is beyond criticism. Of course, you will never know as much about their business as clients do themselves, however you must know sufficient to do a good job and know as much as clients expect you to know — or more. Without this you will simply not be taken seriously and, at worst, you will lack all credibility. The basis of such knowledge increases with time and experience; at least it should do — we all should learn from experience. The successful professional makes a point of it.

- You have to add to the background knowledge you may initially possess with additional information about each client's current circumstances and their specific needs. Prior research apart, this can only become clear progressively as the meeting and the relationship develop, and needs active noting of what is volunteered and active probing to find out more (the latter will be discussed under the heading Identifying Clients' Requirements in chapter 7).

It is these two kinds of information about clients acting together that provide a powerful basis for what you do at meetings. There is a saying that information is power. In winning business, client information and an understanding of it is a most necessary tool and excellence in this area can differentiate you significantly from competitors.

Remember that your success relates directly to your understanding of clients — put yourself more firmly in their shoes than your competitors and you have an immediate edge.

The power of empathy

Empathy is the ability to put yourself in the other person's position and see things from their point of view. It may be your natural instinct, or you may regard it as a skill to be developed and deployed as necessary throughout the selling process — or a bit of both. Whichever may be the case, empathy is vital and it has already been mentioned under the earlier heading about manner.

There is an additional point about it, however, which is worth taking on board. You do not need just to be empathic to take in and appreciate the client's situation, but to do so in a way in which you are doing so clearly shows. Clients must *feel* that you understand. In property, there is nearly always an advisory connotation (often this is key to the relationship as with an architect or surveyor), and this is something that clients demand or appreciate when it is offered. You may be advising on what, from a range of possibilities you feel is most suitable for the client, or you may be acting as a problem solver, analysing some aspect of your client's business or situation and making recommendations linked to how to proceed. In either case, empathy is a necessary part of the process. For example, practical considerations may mean an architect must advise a client away from their initial vision of something, and make this seem a good thing. When clients say of a particular person "... *they're a good person to do business with ...*" empathy is almost certainly one of the key characteristics they have in mind and appreciate.

Respect clients' views

Never assume that clients will see everything the same way as you do. The world is full of different people and they all have differing views, ideas, prejudices and, in some cases, some or all of these may not be the same as your own. So be it. You can agree to differ. You have to work with clients, but you do not have to like them (although it is better if you do get on with most of them, and certainly you need mutual professional respect). Certainly argument is not the best basis for a successful client relationship. This is especially true of business matters — it may matter less if you, say, support different football teams. Attitudes to their company and product or service, to the standard of quality or service, to finance or time — your perspective on all of them may be different to theirs, but taking their view in your stride may be vital. Unless you can understand their view of, say, financial matters you may never be seen as the sort of person to buy from, even if what you offer suits them.

Working with clients

This is a simple, yet effective, point. Clients do not like to be "sold to". In many cultures, the image of the archetypal sales person is not exactly as many might wish it. In this field, you want your image to be seen as professional; but at worst the client views all those with something to sell with suspicion, seeing them as low level, unprofessional con merchants who will use any trick to sell even inappropriate goods to the unwary if it will swell their commission, and brackets you with them.

The historic reasons for this do not matter; for the most part, such an image is actually long outdated; if it does linger on in any way, your job is simply to dispel it. Some categories to whom this book is directed may have more of a problem here than others and, apologies, estate agents come to mind. A number of things can be done to help: one is certainly the concept of working with the client. You should talk about this specifically, rather than giving any hint that you view the meeting as an opportunity for "doing something to them". Expressions such as: *"Let's go through this together"* and *"Let's take some time to work this out together"* give the right feeling and the right description to the transaction, although they need to be balanced alongside the advisory aspect of what you do. Using this kind of phraseology will help you set the correct tone to a meeting and go a little way to dispelling any of the old myths about the insensitive, high-pressure salesperson if such do still exist.

Client types

All clients are important, but they are not all equal. And what I mean here is the size, actual or potential, of the business they do, or may do, with us. The 19th century Italian mathematician Pareto gave his name to what is called *Pareto's Law*. This has become known as the 80/20 rule; in business it may mean that around 80% of your sales comes from about 20% of your client list, and this may be true also of revenue and profit. The figures are not likely to be exact, but all but the most atypical organisation is likely to exhibit this pattern — so, incidentally, is an individual sales territory. Most larger organisations recognise this and will categorise clients into several groups, A, B, C and D for instance, which reflect size. There may be numbers of reasons for categorisation in terms of systems, organisation and so on, however, the key point here is that different clients need different treatment. Such analysis has various uses: for example it is usually sensible to limit the percentage of business dependent on a small number of large clients, too much of a skew here makes you vulnerable if you lose one.

It is not just that clients are best dealt with a little differently for your convenience, it may be less economic to service a smaller client in the same way as a larger one. Additionally, some larger clients demand a different and, from their perspective, better level of service.

If decisions are well made in this area, and the right package of service and representation is directed at each category, then the success with each will be improved. This has got to be done in a way that links revenue (or potential) to cost, and thus margin, and which tries to match, so far as possible, the needs of both parties. The days of dealing with every client as if they were all the same has long gone for most, although none of this implies ignoring the smaller clients. They may only bring in around 20% of the business but no one wants a 20% drop in business. They too have to be looked after. Matching your approach to client size in this way can pay dividends. Sometimes this is an inherent part of the way business is done: for example, a sole agency arrangement being different from one involving several estate agents.

Always take time to organise and categorise your clients and use this arrangement to inform judgments about how you deal with them, how often you contact them and so on.

Types of buyer

While all clients are individuals and must be treated as such, there are those with different attitudes to making buying decisions and this demands a corresponding difference in the way you deal with them. Sorting such categories in the mind is a good start to being able to deal with all the different types of client you meet in the right kind of way. It provides a manageable basis for dealing with the decisions involved. The following is not intended to be definitive, you may well come across people who do not fit in any of the following categories, but it provides a basis for planning and maybe for devising additional categories of your own.

Certainly, it is possible to categorise clients, at least in a general sense and in a way that helps you to get off on the right foot with them, and run a better meeting thereafter.

The way this is usually represented is shown in Figure 6.1 (p52) contrasting just two differing factors on two axis reflecting clients' attitudes and approaches to buying and sales people.

How to open a sale with type 1 (assertive/cold) clients

- Do not expect a warm welcome.
- Accept their negative attitude, and use your professionalism as a foil.
- Keep small talk to an absolute minimum.
- Emphasise that you are there for sound business reasons.
- Make your opening remarks short and to the point.
- Do not be intimidated.

This produces a list of four types, and they are sufficiently different to demand different approaches. This is best described with reference to their likely differing attitudes to making buying decisions, stated below, in quotes, as a client might describe them.

Type 1: (assertive/cold)
"Sales people cannot be trusted. They are determined to sell me something. I neither want nor need. I must therefore be tough and resistant. The best defence against sales people is offence."

Type 2: (accommodating/cold)
"Sales people cannot be trusted. To defend myself I try to avoid them. I stay as uninvolved as possible."

Type 3: (accommodating/warm)
"Many suppliers seem to be very much alike. Since it doesn't matter to me which one I buy from, I prefer to buy from a person I like and who likes me. I like to try to make friends with all the people I investigate as possible suppliers."

Type 4: (assertive/warm)
"I buy things that have been demonstrated and will benefit my company and myself. I buy from people who prove they can help me, by offering products and a quality of service that exactly satisfies my needs."

Figure 6.1 Different attitudes to the buying process

- Do not try to be clever by using what these people will consider "sales people's ploys".
- Appear to let them take the lead, but demonstrate your control of the interview by attentive listening, note taking, and asking concise, factual and open questions, which will, in fact, help direct the meeting.
- Be firm and polite but never appear subservient.
- Position yourself as confident, professional and calmly determined.

How to open as sale with type 2 (accommodating/cold) clients

- Expect these people to appear cool and distant, and understand that you will be seen as a threat to their security until you have won their trust.

- Be calm, professional and unhurried.
- Avoid pressure tactics.
- Do not say too much during the opening moments of an interview. Let them "size you up" for themselves, and do not cloud their picture of you by being flashy, brash or pushy.
- Some small talk is recommended.
- Do not expect to make a sale on your first visit to these people.
- Emphasise your status as an advisor.

How to open a sale with type 3 (accommodating/warm) clients

- Expect a warm welcome, but understand that these people welcome everyone: their warmth does not necessarily mean you are particularly special.
- Allow them to express their feelings with some small talk, but stay in control and do not let them loose sight of the fact that you are there for business reasons.
- As these people like to feel they belong to select groups, mention as early as possible the involvement your company has had with other comparable, reputable companies.
- Tell them exactly how you would like to structure the meeting (the concept of introducing an agenda mentioned earlier), spelling out your role and theirs.
- Do not appear too officious or clinical especially too early on, or by taking too many notes (always ask permission for this): keep the opening conversational.
- Position yourself as a friendly, expert advisor.

How to open a sale with type 4 (assertive/warm) clients

- Expect a correct and professional greeting with a firm handshake.
- Take your seat unhurriedly and prepare openly for the discussion by taking out of your briefcase any necessary documentation and projecting a business-like air.
- Demonstrate your own professionalism, and understand that these people will expect your acknowledgement of their commercial skills.

- Your opening remarks must be natural (not contrived), short and clearly indicate that you already know a fair amount about their company.
- Do not be dogmatic: they will want you to be flexible so that their ideas and objectives can be accommodated in a joint solution.
- Be prepared to revise your call objectives.
- Avoid a fixed or rigid "standard meeting" approach.
- Position yourself as a creative, experienced problem solver.

Respect of the client's individuality, taking an accurate view of what "type" of client you are dealing with and making a real attempt to "get on their wavelength" early on in the proceedings will always help you in any meeting. Sales technique is not, after all, something to be applied slavishly or by rote, but something to be deployed intelligently case-by-case. The variable that dictates exactly how that deployment should vary is the client. Every client is different; and it is a dangerous mistake to treat them as if they were all alike.

Be considerate of anything and everything that will indicate a caring manner, one that respects the client, their views and their property. Clients will appreciate the attitude this displays. With services remember that the first time someone is able to make a judgment about your professional competence is as you sell to them; this judgment starts early on and small details here can affect how you are seen in a way that lasts throughout discussions.

Respect and use clients' names

Names are peculiarly personal. You did not, in all likelihood, choose your own, but you do like people to get it right and remember it. Using names actually changes the feel of a phrase; consider the difference between:

- *"Right, Peter, what I suggest we do is ..."* and
- *"Right, what I suggest we do is ..."*

The feel of each is different.

In many cultures, including the UK, the habit of remembering and using names is weak. So a few pointers and your developing a real intention to get it right may be useful:

- Listen carefully whenever you are introduced or someone says who they are.
- If it is not clear ask again, and if necessary ask how to spell it. Remember people would rather you got their name right and were interested, than made mistakes or had to ask again later.
- Make a point of using the name in the conversation, not so often that it becomes pedantic, and maybe a little more early on to help your memory.
- Always use the name as you leave or conclude a conversation.
- Make a written note of names at the earliest possible moment, and record also other associated names (for instance, someone's secretary).
- Consider carefully when you use the more familiar form of someone's name, too soon and it may offend, too late and they may consider you over formal. (Remember the old line, *"My name is Smith, John Smith, but you may call me 'Sir'."*). This is most important when there are real differences between people: a young estate agent and an elderly householder, for instance.

People do business when you get down to it, not companies. By using names, you can increase the personal feel you give your own company too: do not say, *"I will get the service people to contact you"* quote a name: *"I will get Mr ... of ..."*. So make every contact as personal as appropriate, and this will give a better feel to the conversations that follow.

All clients are different, and they are different, not least, in their requirements. It is to finding out just what such requirements are that we turn to next.

Identifying Clients' Requirements

As was said earlier: *ready, aim and fire!* is a logical order of action for both the military and those in selling. If preparation equates with "ready", then identifying needs is certainly likely to improve the aim. Being "on target" here means having a clear understanding not just about clients, but relating what you do to their specific and individual needs. Of course, some of these they tend to tell you, but often only briefly, or partially. Good investigative skills are necessary here. Winning business is by no means only about putting over your case and demands not the "gift of the gab" alone, but also the ability to ask questions, to do so in the right way, and to listen to and use the answers to better target the approach that you then deploy and follow as you expound your case and make suggestions.

What clients want

Returning again to the buyer's decision-making thinking referred to earlier, remember that clients have two prevailing feelings when buying or considering buying from a particular professional:

- They feel that *they are the important one in the relationship*. You sometimes hear sales people talking about "the buyer's support", as if there was some reason why people should do business with them just to help them. This is wrong. There is no reason why clients should *support* you; they will do business with you if they decide it is in their interests to do so, and only then. So they are right to see themselves as important, and the way in which they are handled in terms of courtesy, efficiency and appropriateness must reflect this.

- They want *a potential supplier to consider their needs*, and consider their needs to be unique, if only in detail. Selling was described earlier as *"helping people to buy"*. In property especially this is a good definition and suggests strongly that having knowledge of what clients want, exactly what they want and how they want it, is the basis for success in this field of selling. Recognising this is the first step. Of course, you have to find out exactly what needs a particular client has, and use that knowledge to increase the effectiveness of your sales approach.

Need identification techniques

While it is essential that you try to find out from a client what their needs are, questions must be asked carefully. This is true whether you are starting with a blank slate or if a prospective client begins by stating a brief that is, in their view, clear, even then it always needs checking, clarifying and, if the need and opportunity is there, extending. This is an area where often client briefs change, sometimes radically; for instance, architects will well know how people come to them with ideas and then as discussion proceeds the brief changes, perhaps coming to reflect reality better or to take a more dramatic approach to something. Always care is necessary here, because:

- The majority of clients are busy, and do not want you subjecting them to a time-consuming Spanish Inquisition-style of questioning; although, with a major project, they may need persuading that time spent on this process is necessary and worthwhile.
- You need to find out certainly and accurately, indeed it is a task which, successfully achieved, helps you differentiate you from your competitors. Just how much you can differentiate and how important that is will be reviewed later.

So how do you go about this questioning? There are several factors that will make what you do work well. Questions need to be:

- *Accurately phrased*. If a question is not clearly and precisely phrased, ambiguity may bring the wrong answer.

- *Mostly open-ended.* That is questions that cannot be answered by *"yes"* or *"no"*. Thus, *"Tell me exactly how you plan to use our services?"* is better than *"Do you see a cost advantage?"* The first gets them talking, which is why open-ended questions work best, and the second, while it may be answered *"yes"*, which does give you some information, may leave other reasons for considering using you unsaid. Open-ended questions are likely to be the best way of obtaining what may be the considerable amount of information we need, and are most likely to make the process most acceptable to the client. Closed questions (those that can be answered *"yes"* or *"no"*) can be used to vary the conversation and verify more specific details in checklist style.
- *Probing.* That is using a series of linked questions that dig deeper and deeper to pursue a particular line and establish fuller understanding. This is an important technique and warrants reviewing in more detail.

There are four levels of probing questions that can be used:

1. *Background questions.* These produce the basic detail, what kind of company is it? How is it organised? What is its budget? — Whatever the required areas of information may be.

Then there are two probing levels, usually called problem and opportunity questions (although the problem level need not always focus on the negative).

2. *Problem questions.* These begin to show what area of activity the product or service being reviewed is to fit in with.
3. *Implication questions.* These pursue the point raised at the previous level to see exactly what the results of any purchase will be.
4. *Need questions.* This is where you want to be, focusing on the need.

The following example makes the principle clearer. Imagine the beginnings of a conversation between someone with a house to sell and a possible estate agent: questions such as, *How many rooms does it have? Where exactly is it located?* And, *How long have you lived there?* All are background questions, and provide a useful start to the information gathering.

Then a question like: *Are you aiming for a quick sale?* Followed by *Why is that?* takes things to the next level. Let us assume that the questioner discovers that the potential seller has a house to buy in mind and young children who would benefit from not missing the start of a new term at a school in their new area. Useful information and if followed up by an implication question, *Does this mean you can be a little flexible on price?*, puts the questioner on strong ground. Finally, a need question focuses the client's mind: *So, if I could suggest a marketing plan that might work fast, but still maximise the price you get for your house, would that hit the spot?* If the estate agent can then do just that, suggesting a plan that sounds practical, then the client will surely take notice.

I heard a similar example recently from friends planning to build on to their house. The conversation went roughly like this:

Architect: What are your reasons for wanting to build onto the house?
Householder: I guess when we moved here we downsized a bit too much and we just need more space.
A: What kind of space exactly, what's it going to be for? (*background*)
H: Well the main thing is to create a study. There is a sort of computer corner in the living room, but it reduces the useful space in that room too much.
A: When we spoke you mentioned that the extension should run off the living room, now I see the room mightn't that cause problems of access to the garden: out of the living room into the new study and then out of the garden? (*problem*)
H: I guess so, the double doors out from the study will take up most of the back wall and we also want a lot more bookshelves.
A: And you were talking about having a put-you-up bed in the study, weren't you, might this just not create the space you want? (*implication*)
H: Yes, that could be.
A: So, if we could position the new room so that access from the living room to the garden was still possible and extend the living room at the same time, would that be likely to give you the increase in space you want? (*need*)
H: Well, yes, what do you suggest?

The classic phases of this sequence are shown.

Never skimp this finding-out process. If it is well done it makes everything you have to do during the remainder of the selling process easier. And if you are in competition and find out the salient facts better and more accurately than anyone else, you should have an edge on them throughout the rest of the process. Of course, this may simplify matters too much: but even the complexity of a surveyor, say, trying to organise representing a client in some major planning application, the principles are the same.

Finding out about clients and obtaining more and better information than your competitors gives you an immediate edge, one that cannot be overestimated; it is one that lasts throughout the sales call. Make getting into this position a priority, and remember in many circumstances it is as much about *clarifying* a brief as it is about finding out from scratch.

Listen to what the buyer says

Listening is always important throughout a meeting. This is reviewed here, as it is especially vital when questioning to identify client needs is taking place. You will look at least careless, and at worst incompetent, if you say something later in the meeting that makes it clear that you have not been listening properly to what a client has said. Listening is easier said than done, there may be many distractions and your mind is necessarily on a number of things at once: what to say next, what to ask and so on. There is an old saying that mankind was made with two ears and one mouth and that that is the right proportion in which to use them, so you must listen carefully and that means what is called active listening. Some ideas about this follow in checklist style:

Active listening: checklist

1. *Want to listen*: This is easy once you realise how useful it is to the sales process.
2. *Look like a good listener*: If they can see they have your attention, clients will be more forthcoming.
3. *Understand*: It is not just the words but what lies behind them that you must note.
4. *React:* Let them see you have heard, understood and are interested. Nods, small comments, and gestures will encourage people to keep talking.
5. *Stop talking*: Other than small comments, you cannot listen and talk simultaneously. Do not interrupt.
6. *Use empathy*: Put yourself in the other person's shoes and make sure you really appreciate their point of view.
7. *Check*: If necessary, ask questions to clarify matters as the conversation proceeds. An understanding based, even partly, on guesses is dangerous. But ask diplomatically, do not say, *You did not explain that very well*.
8. *Remain unemotional*: Too much thinking ahead (How will 1 cope with that objection?) can distract you.

9. *Concentrate*: Allow nothing to distract you (even when walking round a building site).
10. *Look at your clients*: Nothing is read more rapidly as disinterest than an inadequate focus of attention.
11. *Note particularly the key points*: Edit what you are told to make what you need to retain manageable.
12. *Avoid personalities*: It is the ideas and information that matters, not what you think of the person; this can distract.
13. *Do not lose yourself in subsequent argument*: Some thinking ahead may be necessary (you listen faster than they talk, so it is possible); too much and you suddenly find you have missed something.
14. *Avoid negatives*: To begin with at least, signs of disagreement (even visually) can make the client clam up.
15. *Make notes*: see below.

All the above will help you listen more and miss less; and both can make a difference, even being able to play back small things demonstrates how seriously you are taking the client's views.

Making notes

A great deal of information can be obtained in a short time with effective questioning techniques, too much to trust to your memory; however good you may think it to be. You must make notes as you go along. The need for this is compounded by the fact that you often do not know in advance which bits of the plethora of information coming to light will be useful as the meeting progresses, and the relevance of specific points may only become clear as the meeting progresses.

In some meeting situations it may be appropriate to ask for permission before writing down something a prospect says. Organise yourself too to do this conveniently as you move around (maybe inspecting a building), with a clipboard perhaps. All this may seem obvious, but many have walked out of a meeting and immediately had to ask themselves, "*What was it he said?*" — so make a note.

Agreeing needs

Finding out what clients want, exactly what they want and why (and keeping a note of it) is important. However, it is one thing for you to find out, and find out accurately, what your clients want, it is another for them to know that you have done so. Unless they are aware that you have an accurate picture of their requirements they will never develop the same confidence in what you say or recommend. In that case, the usefulness of what you have discovered will be reduced.

The answer is to agree with the client that the needs are true reflections of what the client has said. This can be done with simple questions: *Is that right? Am I understanding you correctly?* Alternatively, it can be done by summarising: *Let me just be sure I have got this right, what you are saying is ...* , listing the key points that have emerged. This makes sure you are correct, and it makes that accuracy of understanding clear to the client. It also allows you to refer back to points in the right way when they are referred to again later in the conversation. It will give a better impression to the client to say: *This will give you the cost effectiveness you said was so important ...* when you refer to the way your product or service will suit them, than if you say: *This will be cost effective, which I am sure you will appreciate ...* . In the latter case, your own certainty may be justified in the case of cost effectiveness, something most people want, but it may be unwise to make too many assumptions about more specific matters.

Regularly use the client's words as an integral part of your conversation and description, it helps link what you say to their feelings and needs and so sharpens your sales effectiveness.

Two kinds of need

There are more client needs than the rest of the space in this book could list. Some are generic; many clients want value for money, efficiency or to save money. Indeed, the same thing can be bought by different clients for very different reasons. The needs one person has for something may not be even remotely the same even for what are very similar clients. Consider a general example, that of holidays. The same resort may be chosen to:

- Provide a romantic break or honeymoon.
- Indulge in sporting activities.
- Meet old friends — or make new ones.
- Work quietly.
- Impress the neighbours, or get away from them.

You can doubtless think of more. Such needs may be tangible or intangible. Similarly, a new car may be bought to fit in the garage (a tangible need for something less than a maximum size); or because it has good fuel economy, which can also be measured. Or it may be to meet a need for an aspiring businessman to look successful; or a younger person to look trendy, both of which are more difficult to specify. Similarly in property, the most important thing about an architect might be a reputation for very modern design; one that a client thinks will impress friends of colleagues rather than being strictly necessary to the job in hand.

There are two key implications here for the sales process:

- First, do not overlook intangible needs. They can be very important to people and may not only be overlooked, but are sometimes not taken seriously by sales people who do not share the need or even understand it.
- Second, and perhaps more importantly, intangible matters can become deciding factors when competition is evenly matched, and buyers search for something to assist them to make a final decision. They do assess the tangible factors, but find this only narrows it down to, say, two possible contenders. At this point, they may well be influenced towards a final choice by something intangible or even just the overall image (of an organisation or of people), things involving much less objective judgments. In conversation, if you recognise that this stage is being reached, then you must focus as much on the intangible as the tangible; perhaps exclusively so.

In taking steps to identify needs both kinds must be sought and the implications to the possible course of the conversation recognised.

Identifying and agreeing client priorities

Before the identification stage is complete, you must ascertain something about clients' priorities. This is important because their various needs often seem straightforward but can, in fact, be in conflict. For instance, a client may say clearly that they want a service supplied:

- fast
- to high quality
- at the lowest possible price.

All this may be unrealistic from any supplier, with something available fast and of high quality being relatively expensive, and something less expensive taking longer to supply. Which factor is the most important? Superficially, the answer may be that all three criteria are important. Further questioning can discover that, if a choice has to be made, cost is regarded as being most important. Or perhaps timing is the key and the client's attitude to cost will change to achieve what they want in this area. How you best proceed is radically altered by such priorities: imagine, for instance, the differences posed for an estate agent when told to sell a property either *at the highest possible price* or *as quickly as possible*. Similarly, the legal situation posed in trying to get an unruly tenant to move out may change depending on the importance of timing versus costs or compensation.

As with needs themselves, the identified priorities can be agreed with the client and any reference back made in their terms: *"So, your priorities will be met, achieving completion ahead of that deadline and ..."*.

As your product or service will only be acceptable to the client if it meets their priorities, this identification is crucial. Without it everything else done can be off target, if priority identification is achieved accurately the case you go on to describe is then more likely to fit in neatly with their requirements.

Using client records

Although client records should be originated early on in any relationship with a new client, and act as a reminder of basic details such as the client's name and address, their use goes far beyond this simple role. They can help ensure that your approach is accurately directed, and tailored to the needs of every individual client. So the record will, if made to contain the right information, act as a checklist to remind you of a multitude of facts about the client. Without doubt clients want an individual approach, they want their particular needs met and rightly believe that these are unique. Perhaps they are. Even if not, small differences between the requirements of one client and another will be important to them. It is easy to pretend that we retain every detail about something so important as a list of clients, but most of us do not have perfect memories. You really do need a written record of any facts that will help you sell more effectively, and a check, albeit brief, of the records should be made a mandatory action prior to every call.

This is certainly an action point, one that many people skimp on. Create good, accurate, clear records. Keep them up to date and use them as a sales aid to make your selling more effective.

Having touched on the subject of client records, some of the other topics that can usefully be used to record are listed here:

- Client's name, address, telephone, e-mail, fax etc.
- Contact names and job titles.
- Account number.
- Source of original lead.
- Record of business done (including different things bought and value).
- Contact frequency and timing.
- Personal details (client preferences — even their birthday).
- Geographical details (where exactly are they, can you park easily nearby).
- Client organisation background (subsidiaries, other locations etc).
- Financial details (discounts, special arrangements etc).
- Potential and trends.

You can no doubt extend and refine this list with your own business in mind. Remember, as you do decide what to record, that you are creating a *company* record (they are only your clients on behalf of the company) and the degree of detail is, in part, dictated by what *others* need to know. A morbid thought perhaps, but ask yourself what would happen if you had an accident and someone had to pick up the thread on client relationships for which you have responsibility. The information recorded should make this as easy as possible.

The record card is a useful aid to sales effectiveness and sales productivity; it deserves careful utilisation.

Now, with all that has gone before in mind, we turn to the way in which you make the case for what you want — and make it persuasive.

Presenting
Your Case 8

This is the heartland of the sales process: *the persuasive core of every meeting*.

Whatever else needs to be done, and whatever else may exert influence over the degree of impact you have, there is a major job to be done here. It is here that you must be most specifically persuasive, yet there is more to it than that. Whatever you must do to put across your case (this can include description, illustration and demonstration) must be done carefully in a way that increases the power of the picture you are building up in the client's mind. You must also continue to differentiate, as it is here that clients are making their most direct comparisons with your competitors. Always assume there *are* competitors incidentally, and never assume they are anything but professional. The factors reviewed in this chapter are all directed at increasing the effectiveness of what you do in this central area of the business-winning task.

What it means to be persuasive

Clients want to make a buying decision *their* way. They want to think about whatever proposition you are making to them, they want to assess it and make what they would regard as a considered decision. Their thinking is designed, however consciously, to weigh up the case (see figure 8.1) putting many points of differing import on the scales, as it were, to see how the whole picture stacks up (and, of course, if they are comparing you with competition then it is two or more such balances which they will look at, comparing one against the other).

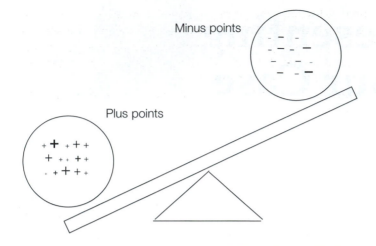

Figure 8.1 Weighing up the case

The thinking involved can be characterised as follows, in a sequence first formalised by psychologists in the US, which you will find mirrors a common sense analysis of what goes on in the buyers' mind (think of your own thoughts as you contemplate some purchase). This was set out earlier and is worth repeating here. It showed buyers saying to themselves:

- *I am important* — they want to be treated as such.
- *Consider my requirements* — they want to be dealt with as a unique individual.
- *How do I know your proposition will help me?* — they want details, explanation, description and proof.
- *What are the facts?* — they want to put together a picture that enables them to make a decision.
- *What are the snags?* — nothing is perfect, and most purchases involve compromise, so these points must be discovered, assessed and added appropriately to the balance.
- *How do we do business?* — they also want to assess how it will all work, who will they deal with, whether deadlines will be met, communications will be clear, what about service and so on.
- *I agree* — but only if their analysis leads them to that conclusion.

A professional sales approach must take this thinking process into account and match the thinking. Remember selling may be sensibly described as helping people to buy, but it must also be persuasive, your approach must work for you as well as fit the prospect's thinking. So what do we mean by "persuasive"?

We can define "persuasive" as a communications approach that is seen by the client as being:

- understandable
- attractive
- convincing.

None of these on their own is enough to secure business, and together they must not only make a strong case to the client, but also they must differentiate your case from competition and do so powerfully enough to make you, your product or service and company first choice. As we have seen, selling must be based on client needs, and identifying these is a priority; using them is a priority too. There is no point in asking the client a great many questions and then manifestly not appreciating their situation as you go on to explain in detail what your product or service offers. In most fields of property selling clients expect a tailored approach.

Perhaps the first rule here is that your approach must be individually tailored to give each and every client what they want, an approach that respects their point of view, which matches their needs and so generates more immediate interest.

Bearing this in mind will get you off on the right track and will quickly show the reason why needs identification and preparation are so important. But this is a complex stage; there are many disparate things to be done; yet the whole stage must proceed smoothly. This is important to your personal positioning: if it is handled smoothly, if it appears well thought out and relevant (because it is!), then the client will conclude they are dealing with a professional and take more serious note of what you say.

Now, we consider in turn the three key criteria that, together, create persuasiveness and how you can put them to work.

1. Making what you say understandable

It is probable that more sales are lost because of lack of understanding than for any other more complex reason. This is certainly true of a specialist and technical area such as property. And the reason is simple; communication is not easy. The chance of misunderstanding is ever present between two people with different backgrounds, experience, intentions, prejudices and points of view. This may involve the different interpretation of one word — for example, just how fast is *immediately*? This may mean that someone will see to something when they are in the office tomorrow morning and post the details that day. Someone else may assume they will have the details by e-mail within the hour. Alternatively, it may be that a long disjointed explanation of, say, the cost advantages offered ends up confusing rather than informing.

The first rule is probably to be careful, not falling into the trap of thinking that communication is entirely straightforward, but making sure that you choose words carefully and make sure that you work at being clearly understood. Similarly, avoid repeating slavishly out of pure habit a standard version that is not fully tailored. Remember too that people are really impressed by good explanation: something that they expect to be complicated but which turns out to be straightforward. This is a sound basis for a good impression, and for positioning yourself as an expert. What else helps guarantee that there is understanding? I would mention four factors:

1. *Structure*: the logic of any message is crucial. This means taking things one at a time, in bite-sized pieces that both you can deal with manageably and that the client can comprehend, and flagging or "sign posting" what is being done. Thus something that begins, *You will want to know about how we can meet your needs, what costs are involved and how quickly things can be up and running. Let's take your needs first, then I'll say something about the finances, then ...* is likely to be followed more easily than something that just jumps in and deals with points at random. If the client knows what is coming and feels it will be what they want to hear they will be more receptive, indeed knowing your initial thinking is clear and appropriate impresses and gives some advance credence to what is to come. The antithesis, what I call the "and another thing" approach, where what is said is apparently at random and unprepared, much less designed to be appropriate to the individual, is much less powerful and may fail to make a case at all.

2. *Sequence*: this goes logically with structure. There needs to be a clear and relevant sequence to the way that you go through something and, again, this should be clear to the client. For

instance, an estate agent needs to decide a logical route to show people around a house highlighting key aspects of it and linking things together along the way. Every meeting needs thinking about, and organising, in this way to make sure that one, two, three does not become two, three, one.

3.   *Visual (or sales) aids*: something visual always makes things easier to understand. The estate agent has the whole property to act as a visual aid, indeed many of the people we are focusing on here have the same advantage; an architect is another example. But much simpler things have the same effect. A picture is worth a thousand words the old saying has it, and there is a great deal of truth in it. A graph may make a point about cost effectiveness in a moment, when it might otherwise take many minutes to explain; photographs, charts, brochures, all these will help you get your message across.

4.   *Description*: Do not just tell people something; paint them a picture. Some property people rarely use an adjective, yet it is essential that people see what you mean. You must stir their imagination. An extension on a house is not going to create a *nice space*, it is going to *transform living arrangements*. Help with planning permission is not just going to be *a bit* easier, it is going *remove all the hassle and smooth the path of the project*. While you need to beware of becoming clichéd (and some, like estate agents, must be particularly careful: first because some of their terminology has reached classic joke status, and second because the need to stimulate imagination is high), but it is worse to sell yourself short by failing to create a real picture in the buyer's mind and thus generate full understanding. Bland language can do just that, diluting the impression you want to give by default. It is not a very good approach — let us rephrase that: it is a disastrous approach that can kill the prospects of gaining agreement stone dead.

In presenting your case, this aspect rightly comes first; understanding is the foundation upon which the rest of the selling process rests.

Beware of jargon

Nothing dilutes understanding more easily than inappropriate use of jargon. Jargon is professional slang and is particularly used in context of technical matters. Between people of like understanding it is a useful shorthand. Within my own firm no one has time to say *"all comers' seminar"* (meaning a training event promoted by, say, a management institute and attended by people from several different organisations) so we say *"GT course"*. It stands for general training course, we all know what it means and using it saves a second or two. It is meaningless, however, to our clients and such a phrase must not be used externally or it will cause confusion. What is worse you may not detect such confusion. People do not always react at once to such a phrase. They do not interrupt and ask what it means (not least because they may fear they should know and do not wish to appear stupid). They let it go by and hope the overall sense of what is being said remains clear. But if it happens often, they notice; and quite possibly their understanding is reduced, or they do get lost, have to ask and resent the need to do so. Either way, your credibility suffers.

So watch out for jargon, especially as for most people its use is a habit. It comes in two varieties:

- organisational jargon
- industry jargon.

Corporate jargon used within an organisation, such as I quoted above, often reduces things to sets of initials — these describe the products, systems, processes, people, departments, all the things to which reference is made often and where a shorthand description is therefore useful, *provided that everyone understands it.*

The technicalities of an industry also give rise to jargon; some more than others. Computers are a case in point, one with which we are probably all familiar. The machine on which I prepared this book is a marvel of modern technology. But its manual has a nightmare lack of clarity. The language in it seems to be 90% jargon and assumes that the user has a particular level of understanding that makes this appropriate, this despite the fact that it would be perfectly possible to write most of it in plain English. This makes a good final point: the important thing with jargon is not so much to avoid all the technicalities, but to make absolutely sure that they are pitched at an appropriate level for those to whom you speak; each of them individually. In addition, some phrases become so hackneyed that they lose all meaning. I once asked a friend in the computer world what exactly the phrase *"user friendly"* meant, he thought for a moment, then said: *"I suppose it means it is very, very complicated, but not as complicated as next year's model!"*. Some descriptions just get past their sell-by date, as it were. User friendly might once have been a neat description, these days it has been applied to everything and fails to add any real power.

Every aspect of the property world has its own jargon and a range of people to be dealt with at differing levels of technical competence; so an important thing here is to match the level used to the person involved.

To use (but also explain!) some jargon of jargon: adopt a NUJA approach (that is: never use jargon automatically). It can be useful, but it may dilute understanding and its use needs some conscious thought.

2. Make what you say attractive

It is one thing to be understood, it is another to make your descriptions truly attractive so that clients want to listen and are keen to let you complete the case. So, how do you do this?

The base principle here is that clients do not buy products and services for what they *are*, they buy them for what the products or services *do for them or mean to them* — for their *benefits*. To take a general example, people do not buy precision drills (what they are), but the ability to make precision holes (what drills will do); and they will only want that because of some deeper need, to repair the car or put up shelves.

This is probably the single most important tenet of successful selling, yet the world over there are many people talking predominantly about *features*, things that the product or a part of it is, when they should be talking benefits. As a result, there are too many buyers with their eyes glazing over saying to themselves *"So what?"*.

Talking benefits, and indeed leading with benefits, is key in making what you say attractive. It is not so complicated, yet perhaps because so many property people learned about what they sell from the starting point of the technicalities (and often in the property world through technical qualifications), it is somehow most natural to talk about features — it can take conscious effort to state things the other way round.

The first task is to recognise which is which, feature or benefit, and it is useful to think through your product/service listing benefits first and see how they link with features. Consider a simple example: a car may have a five-speed gearbox (a feature), telling the client this may seem just like another piece of technical information prompting the response *"So what?"*. Worse the inexperienced driver may worry that it is more complicated than he can manage. If the sales person has identified a need for economy, he can talk first about low fuel usage and money saved (benefits), quoting the feature of the five-speed gearbox as a reason that makes that possible. One feature may, of course, link to more than one benefit. In the case of the car, reduced engine wear and smoother, quieter high-speed cruising may also result from the five-speed gearbox. Try thinking this through with something a little more technical in mind (ABS brakes or torque, perhaps for the car) or applying it to your own situation.

All the description you use can be handled in this way. As a result avoid the use of phrases that mean a lot to the person who uses them, but which fail to explain the full meaning to clients. For instance: *an estate agent may claim to have wide coverage of the area. Meaning what exactly — a very large flat office spread over an acre? No: what they would probably say, if made to extend the point, is that they have: an extensive chain of offices, use all suitable newspapers to advertise locally (and maybe nationally as well), so that more people see the details, are prompted to make contact to obtain more information and arrange a viewing and that chances of a sale, breaking the chain and being able to move before the start of the next school term are high.* This is not suggested as the exact way of saying it, rather to make the point that the first part is actually describing features, and only as it is explained does the description turn to focus on benefits and become both inherently more interesting and more closely linked to the need of the client. The tendency to allow short statements to do the job of a better explanation is a common way of ensuring that the power to persuade is short-changed; beware.

Talking benefits in this way as you describe the product, company, people and service that support them is a vital part of the sales job. It is important to get it right; you should not be talking about a room (in an office) that has a particular square foot/metre dimension, but perhaps about a room that is of a size, *that will allow the design department to be housed together and link conveniently to production.*

Remember all clients are different and, in some cases, you may be selling to a group of people who *all* have influence on a decision, as with a board of directors. In either case, people will have their own needs and agenda and benefits must be presented so that they relate to all these individual situations and points of view.

Relating benefits to individual clients

The tailored nature of the approach necessary in this field has been mentioned before. Linked to benefits it is vital. It is one thing to define what the various benefits or features are, but that does not mean you have to throw all the benefits indiscriminately at every client. Two things are important here: suitability and comprehensiveness.

- *Suitability*: In the example of a motorcar, fuel economy was shown as a benefit assisted by the feature of a five-speed gearbox (this is not the only contributor to the level of fuel use, of course). However, the usefulness of this benefit depends on the individual customer being interested in economy. Someone buying a high-performance, prestige car, such as a Ferrari, might not care how far it goes on a litre of fuel, although they could be interested in other benefits produced by the same feature — high-speed cruising being more comfortable in a fifth gear. So benefits must always be selected intelligently to match client needs and priorities.
- *Comprehensiveness*: I once called on a client accompanying someone working for a surveying firm. Early on in the meeting the client asked: *"Perhaps you could give me some background about your company?"* — *"Certainly"*, came the reply, following which they did not appear to draw breath for 35 minutes. He described chronologically the company history, its start, development, ups and downs, the people, clients, services — ad nauseum. Each piece of information was well described, it was all true, but most of it was simply irrelevant to the client, who had probably expected 35 sentences, or even words, rather than 35 minutes. Comprehensiveness is never, or rarely, an objective; achieving comprehensiveness just takes too long. Clients are busy people and they expect you to concentrate on what is most important — to them.

    You must have all sorts of information at your fingertips in terms of benefit, but you must then select from it, picking those benefits which you judge are most likely to make the case you want, and using those, in the right order and the correct way, to achieve what you want and do so succinctly. Do this and your proposition will seem more attractive to more people.

Deploying different types of benefits

There are three different types of benefits and each presents different opportunities to make what you sell appear attractive. These are:

- *Benefits to the person in their job*. Thus a survey allows a property developer to get on with refurbishment, content that there are no hidden horrors likely to blight their project.
- *Benefits to the client as a person*. The survey above may also allow the developer to justify a decision to buy to their boss.
- *Benefits to others who are important to the client*. Thus, the survey helps the contractor hired by the developer to estimate the time the work will take.

Using the full range of benefits available and relating them to all possible types of need can increase the power of what you say. So too can combining this sort of statement into a logical sequence so that all the listener's needs are met.

For example, someone (an estate agent) might say: *The advertisement we recommend is (size) and includes a photograph (feature). This means it is most likely to be seen and gives sufficient information to prompt enquiries (benefit). Thus, you get viewers with a real interest coming along promptly and increase your chances of a quick sale (benefit and need satisfaction).*

The more you work with the concept of benefits, the more adept you will become to putting things in the terms with which clients most readily identify.

Time and care spent on getting the core description of what you sell right — focused on what it will *do for* the (individual) client — is vital. Without this any description will be pedestrian and unlikely to top competitive offerings; with it you have an immediate competitive edge.

3. Make what you say credible

In defining persuasion, the third element mentioned was making what is said convincing and credible to the client. Most would appreciate the truth of the fact that the client has some inherent scepticism towards anyone selling. They believe that you have a vested interest, they believe that they need to be sceptical and if a good point is made about your product or service, their first reaction may be to think: *"They would say that, wouldn't they"*. So they want proof.

The main form of evidence, certainly the one that builds in best to the benefit-orientated conversation you should be conducting, is the features. Well-selected benefits on their own reflect client needs. Benefits followed by features reflect needs and offer linked proof, as in a statement such as: *"This model will give you the low fuel consumption you want and reduce your motoring costs, because it has a five-speed gearbox"*. There is factual, physical proof here; the client can see and touch the gear lever, and is reassured that it really exists and it is not just a sales ploy. Such proof may be asked for and, even if it is not, should be built into the argument you are putting across as it is an inherent requirement of the buyer. Never rely solely on your own argument, build some real proof into the case you present.

More proof may be needed than can be provided by features alone and, in particular, clients may demand that this is from some outside source, independent of whoever they are dealing with and their organisation. Here you may need to do some assembling of the kind of point that can be made to offer such *external* proof. There are different independent authorities to be quoted in different fields. For instance, the following are sources of independent opinion and thus provide proof:

- An award received by an architect.
- A link with another respected entity: between a surveyor and an insurance company or an architect and a planning consultant.
- Sales figures may have this impact: the estate agent with the greatest number of sales in the area.
- Experience similarly: 20 years in business (and the time can be independently checked) may mean something in terms of quality or reliability.
- Positive editorial comment in the trade press and other media.

You need to think systematically about your own organisation to assemble all possible proof factors that can then be kept in mind and used when appropriate.

A further, and sometimes more powerful, form of proof is that of testimonials or references; in other words, past or current clients. Even general mention of the people you already deal with to a potential new buyer can be reassuring. Specific past names quoted may be more useful. Remember you may need to obtain permission; are other clients happy for their names to be mentioned? Is any confidentiality involved? And select carefully. Quoting to a small company that you do business with several large multinationals may put them off, and vice versa. Similarly, if you quote a company that is competitive with another, this may just annoy them, and if they are so dissimilar that they feel they cannot compare this may add nothing. Work and clients go together: for example, an architect might be able to quote their work creating a public, or simply visible, building believing that it will impress — if they did that, they must be good.

The correct supporting evidence, fielded in the right way, is powerful in adding credibility and strengthening differentiation. Have the right evidence ready and use it wisely (in many fields of property direct examination acts as a credibility-boosting factor).

Beyond these three key elements there are various further techniques that are useful to ensure putting over your case during a meeting goes well.

(i) *Checking progress*

The stage of any meeting when you are describing your offering is one when, perhaps necessarily, you will be doing most of the talking; but you should *not* be doing it all. You need to have some feedback as the meeting progresses to check that you are on target. It is easy to let your enthusiasm for getting across your message make you talk uninterrupted, yet the client will not value a monologue so much as a conversation in which they are involved. They appreciate your checking periodically whether you still have their interest and whether what you are saying continues to be relevant.

This is easily done, in part, by observation. Obvious signs of acceptance or rejection you will see at once provided you look for them. Nods, expressions and manner will all provide clues as to what reaction you are getting. But you need more than this, your conversation has to include checks such as: *"Does that make sense?"*, *"Should I give you more details of that?"*. Such questions need not be complicated, and if some of them are open questions, that is the client cannot answer them with a simple yes or no, then you will obtain actual comment as to how they are feeling. Asking, for example, *"How well does what I am saying tie in with the kind of approach you have in mind?"*. Not only is the feedback valuable, but the information provided is like having a hand on the tiller in a boat, enabling gentle changes of course as the voyage progresses and as conditions change along the way. The whole process improves the accuracy of what you do and the likelihood of agreement resulting from it.

(ii) *Summarise progress*

Perhaps an extension of checking progress is the technique of summarising. This is always useful, but the longer your typical sales meeting is, and the more complicated it may be, then the greater the need to keep it well organised. If you are directing the meeting and proceeding in a clear, structured manner, then the client should keep up with the argument; however, summarising briefly as you go along will help make sure everything remains clear throughout. You do not want to give the impression of extending the meeting unnecessarily, but you do need to recap, especially on topics that are important. This can be done as a help to both parties and sign posted as exactly what it is: *"Let me just summarise at this point, it seems there are three main criteria that have to be met, first, ..."*. Or you can make it a part of the conversation. In either case, it will help the meeting to stay on track and keep things straight in your mind. Keep the client with you in this way; it can help keep them with you right up to the moment they say "yes".

(iii) Managing sales aids

A sales aid is any physical element used to enhance what is said. Here we consider their use, but first how do you store them? In a word: carefully. Many times I have seen people who have either been unable to find something they have said they will show the client, or who have pulled it from a briefcase that looks as if it contains the aftermath of a small explosion. Such inefficiency will be noticed. Sales aids are important and they deserve to be looked after.

Sales aids also need to be used correctly and the golden rule is that you must let them speak for themselves. There are two things many people find difficult in dealing with clients; being patient and keeping silent. And the good use of sales aids demands both. For example, if someone is showing details of a building, their use demands a systematic approach:

- They must first be *introduced*. This introduction should explain why it is being shown, in other words what it will help explain to the client — and why they will find it helpful.
- Then you *show* them. And you wait. You wait until the client's attention comes back to you from the picture, plans or whatever, because, if the thing is of any interest at all, then when it is put in front of them they will want to look at it, which will take their attention. A client cannot look at something, concentrate on it, and listen to you at the same time. And the more complex or the more interesting it is, the longer you must remain waiting silently. This

may seem a simple point, but because it can seem awkward to keep silent there is a temptation to continue the conversation. But if you do, and if what you say is an important point, you may succeed only in distracting from the visual and yet not do so sufficiently for someone to take in the point you have just made. After a moment's hiatus, the conversation resumes and not as good a total point has been made as you would have wished. This scenario is made more complicated if you have, say, a whole brochure or portfolio to go through, every time you turn over a page then you must wait for the client to take in what they see and for their attention to return to you.

- Then you *remove* it, so that it does not distract as you continue speaking (promising to leave a copy of it if this is desirable) and continue the meeting.

The effect of seeing something at a sales meeting is powerful. The client finds things easier to understand. And this, of course, they notice and value. It helps paint a picture, and it can save time — a commodity that the client will doubtless value. It also adds variety to the meeting, which helps maintain concentration.

Furthermore, such aids can appear very personalised. Something may be shown to the client as what is clearly part of the standard sales material, something all or most clients see. Nothing wrong with that, the client will expect the sales person to be well equipped in this respect and likes to see that they are. But sometimes there is an opportunity for material to create a different impression by being (or sometimes seeming to be) tailored just for this one client. This may come in the description: *"Knowing we would need to talk through the figures, I prepared a graph that will ..."*. Or it may be visually tailored; material prepared using the client's figures perhaps, or a note to be left with them that has their name or company logo on it.

Good sales aids can help the client find the meeting memorable. It pays dividends to make sure that you have the right number of them, that they are good quality and appropriate — that is genuinely helpful to the client — and to use them carefully and effectively.

Note: So important is it to get things right in this area — the correct aids, appropriately organised — that it may be useful to list what you plan to use in a checklist. Listing the items you have to deploy, and linking them to such factors as:

- The client situation they best relate to.

- What aspect of what you will say they illustrate.
- Proof that what you say is true.

(iv) Do not exaggerate

This is a most important maxim. Never, ever exaggerate. Nothing switches a potential client off more quickly than obvious over exaggeration; do not be tempted to do it. One phrase too many and your credibility collapses around you, in fact of all the mistakes you can make in selling this is ... but you are right, I am exaggerating. Although, I hope to make a point.

Credibility is a fragile flower and a good case can easily be diluted by something that strikes a potential client as "over the top". If you have a good offering by all means say so, but give reasons for excellence and spend more time talking more about what something does for or means to the particular client than about simply the fact that it is good. Beware particularly of superlatives. If you say something is *"the best"* then you must be able to back it up. Too strident a description from which you have to climb down: *"Well, when I say best, I mean undoubtedly one of the best ..."* will dilute any favourable impression you may initially have achieved. Remember the scepticism with which much of what anyone with something to sell is received, and that clients question each statement, asking themselves whether it should be taken at face value, whether it is to be believed and deciding whether the case being presented is becoming stronger or weaker. Finally, remember that few things are "unique" (a much overused word meaning literally like nothing else); and that being quite, very or entirely "unique" is simply grammatically incorrect and a misuse of a useful word, which is powerful when correctly used.

(v) Do not pressurise

Clients prefer to make a considered judgment to buy. Pressure to make a decision before they have completed what they regard as the necessary thinking process, weighing up the pros and cons of a potential purchase, will often have the reverse effect of that desired. It will increase their resolve to think it through and not to be rushed. Undue pressure is usually read in three ways:

- As insensitivity to the client's point of view (this is particularly bad because one of the things they positively seek as a characteristic of professional people is understanding of them and their point of view).

• As a smoke screen for some weakness in your case, which they feel will show itself in time, hence the inappropriate rush to close the deal.

• As desperation, which might have all sorts of causes — none of which inspire confidence in a buyer and make you appear unprofessional.

So go for a successful outcome by all means, push hard, be persistent, but do not put undue pressure on the client in a way that will be obvious and which will be read as unprofessional.

(vi) Demonstrating effectively

Not everything lends itself to demonstration, but many do (if yours is not one such, by all means skip on). Where called for, an effective demonstration can strengthen the overall presentation considerably, and is another area to potentially strengthen differentiation. Seeing is believing. There is no substitute for a client having the evidence of their own eyes to back up what is said. But demonstrations must be approached in the right way; they must be effective and that means 100% effective. Anything less simply does not meet the need.

An effective demonstration starts with consideration of to whom you are demonstrating. It may be to one person; it may be to several. A group situation illustrates some of the problems of a formal presentation. You may feel exposed standing in front of an expectant group, and thinking beforehand about what you will say and how you will make it go smoothly and boost your self-confidence. Is the decision maker there? Or are you talking to someone who will make recommendations to someone else? This may be important to how you direct things, similarly, and perhaps more important still, are you talking to the user? Imagine showing a couple and their parents around a house; who is truly most important? Each person may have a different agenda and be looking for, and potentially swayed by, different points.

Let us take a tour of a building as an example (it could be a house or office that is for sale or rent, say). To do it successfully needs preparation. Whatever you are showing needs to be well presented (this may be something you can ensure or that involves persuading the vendor to do). You need all the facts at your fingertips: for instance, if asked how many power points there are in the sitting room, do you know?

What are the key factors? Well, many of the basic rules of selling apply: you must focus on needs, maintain interest (maybe not everything may be of the same level of interest and a comprehensive tour may be neither necessary nor appreciated), go through matters to a pre-explained structure and sequence and, above all, talk benefits. The job is to get people to imagine the place in use (the classic general example is a car and the test drive allows someone to imagine owning and driving it; viewing a house has a similar connotation). With that in mind, remember:

- *Set up fast*: Make sure everything is ready: have you got the key and is the electricity switched on?
- *Make it understandable*: This is vital. Tours can be spoilt by jargon, gobbledegook and confusion; a lengthy discussion about details of construction that are of little interest, perhaps. Everything must be spelt out so that it is crystal clear. Finding it easy to understand will be read as a good sign, and prompts to imagination can quickly build up a powerful picture — *which of the children would you see having this room?*.
- *It must work!* If there is no where to park, the key does not fit the lock or you get an electric shock when you turn on a light then, from the client's point of view, you have a problem, and quite right too. The experience must be as smooth as silk.
- *Make them feel how it could be*: Everything must be done not just so that they "get a feeling for the place" in a general sense, but also so that they can truly imagine how it would be to live or work in it (the detail is important here — you do not want people, on their own later, not appreciating that there was space for the washing machine or something else crucial). This applies even if "could be" needs taking literally, with a viewing of one room accompanied by the comment, *Imagine the size this would be with that wall removed*.
- *Project what you want: And what the client wants.* If the tour must demonstrate comfort, quirkiness, ease of maintenance, or potential for expansion, then make sure such prime messages comes across.

Throughout the process the emphasis is perhaps on proof. You are not just talking about it, you can show it, they can try it — and seeing is believing.

You must work to ensure everything is exactly as you want. There are few second chances in selling and in few parts of the process is this truer than when showing something in this way. Time spent beforehand to make sure that you get it right is time very well spent.

(vii) *Making terms and conditions clear*

Many property businesses have contractual terms of varying degrees of complexity. Sometimes there are factors within them, which clients do not like, however much they understand the necessity for them; cancellation arrangements are perhaps an example of this. Because of the perceived difficulty in introducing such topics, it is easy when selling to avoid facing such issues: the thinking tends to be that it is better first to concentrate on obtaining agreement and then worry about the terms of business. But this can cause problems. Clients can feel that issues have been disguised or avoided rather than delayed, and you need a clear policy as to how you deal with such issues in your business. This needs to be tailored, every business is different in the way terms operate, but some general pointers may be useful.

The existence and use of any terms and conditions must protect the financial position of the supplier and, in particular, protect profitability. At the same time, it is important that they:

- Are communicated clearly and prevent misunderstandings.
- Project efficiency.
- Enhance the client relationship (and thus be seen as acceptable and necessary).
- Encourage conversion of business effectively and promptly.
- Link to any other necessary arrangements and documentation.

In discussing terms and conditions never apologise for their necessity. Stress the *mutual* advantages, talk about working together and, if necessary, use a checklist to ensure you deal with everything systematically. Specifically, you may want to evolve a step-by-step way of introducing, describing and making terms and conditions stick. The following illustrates the kind of progression involved.

- *Introduce the concept of contractual agreement*: You need to consider the timing of this in your business, but it is usually best early on rather than later, and although details may be left over, it is important to make it clear that "contract" is something confirmed in writing. Remember the moment passes; it may become progressively more difficult to introduce contractual matters later once it has been left too long. Do not wait for clients to raise the issue. They are unlikely to do so. And link mention of the contract to the written offer.

- *Make clear the detail*: You must be careful to spell out accurately the detail and should not assume the client is familiar with everything — even if they have dealt with you previously. For example, consultants charging expenses such as travel costs must be clear about how this works (first-class or second on the train, for instance).

- *Stress particularly figures and timing*: There must no misunderstanding about the details which, in the worst scenario, can cause the greatest problem. For example, are costs inclusive of tax? When is, *In a month's time* exactly? (four weeks or ...?). Two factors are of particular importance: deposit policy/timing and credit arrangements. Deal with these thoroughly and carefully.

- *Check understanding*: This may be as simple as an occasional, *Is that clear?* but is very important. It is no good, at a later stage, believing that everything was straight between you — you need to know from the start.

- *Document your side of arrangements:* Tell the client what you will do, and follow it up efficiently and promptly in a way that sets the pattern for clear to and fro written confirmation. And make it easy for the client. Administrative chores breed delay, clients may prefer you to summarise details of a discussion so that they can write a couple of lines that say, *That's right, I agree*. The reverse will take longer. This may be checklist-led, in other words, the details that need to be documented come off an agreed checklist document that acts as a prompt and reminder; it can be all too easy to overlook apparently small details.

- *Ask for confirmation*: Whatever it is you want — written confirmation, a signed contract (as agreed internal policy specifies) — you need to specifically ask for it. It is unnecessary to go round the houses, you do not need to make an issue of it (the client does, after all, see what is happening as a business arrangement and will not be surprised), but you do need to make the process, and implications clear, and get it under way.

- *Record the action*: Keep a clear note of what you have done, how the client has responded and, most important, when it needs checking and when further action is needed. This should clearly link to follow-up diary systems or be, infallibly, a part of the more sophisticated computer database and "prompt" systems that many people use today for their client records and information.

- *Chase for action*: This is crucial. If the client ignores key stages, and some will, you must actively remind them of their commitment. Do not feel awkward about doing this; after all you should be following up agreed commitments (*"when will you let me have the contract back?" "By the end of the week."*) so clients will expect it, and besides the penalty for delay can be very damaging. Such chasing must therefore always be systematic, courteous, but insistent.

- *Adopt the appropriate manner*: Throughout the process make it clear that this is not a negative procedure, indeed, ultimately, it can be presented as a protection for clients. So it is best to deal with it in a way that is efficient, and implies good service, that is professional and, if necessary, positions you as an appropriate point of contact from the client's viewpoint.

- *Link to follow-up*: The contractual arrangement links to all stages of the sale and those beyond. The supplier must deliver "on the day", this is their part of the contract and all the service issues are important here.

Further, we should see the process described as linking to:

- *Invoicing*: Here it is important that the invoice reflects — *accurately* — the agreed detail (and clients can find too often that this is not the case), and is straightforward and clear. This may best be submitted with a personalised covering note linking to obtaining feedback and to the future relationship. Sending the invoice, of course, implies chasing to receive payment. Again not an easy — or palpable — task, but it must be done and it is easier to follow up in a way that gets it seen as a routine, rather than only when so much time has gone by that the approach must be heavy. This is vital. So is cash flow and these days the need to chase is, perhaps regrettably, the norm. (One of my first experiences of sales work was being told: *It's not a sale until the money is in the bank.* Wise advice, even if I digress somewhat.)

- *Selling-on*: As future contact is made and as a relationship is forged, we want the contractual side to become easier. Next time the procedure is "as before", and if all went well this will be seen by the client as reasonable, straightforward and hassle-free.

Anything contractual is an important area to deal with effectively. It is an integral part of much property business. If delayed, skimped or ignored, it will certainly cause problems. Contracts and terms are, after all, primarily for when things go wrong, it is only then that many need to turn to the "letter of the law". Get this area right and it provides a firm basis for profitable business.

(viii) *Do not sound egocentric*

To a degree, setting out to win business inevitably involves an egocentric approach. You have to think of it as *your* meeting, you want — indeed intend — it to be successful, you have to aim for the objective, and that is always ultimately to close the deal and get a commitment (ultimately an order) and this could be described as getting your own way. All true and necessary, yet this approach should not show inappropriately and must not show overtly in your language.

So, do not prefix things you say by, for example: *If you want my opinion ...* , or *If I were you I would ...* . It too easily sounds patronising. Clients may well be interested in your advice, but they expect it to be tailored to them, and based on consideration of their circumstances. It is much better to lead into comments with: *For a company of your size, the best approach is often ...* , or *Given what you said about timing, we might best deal with it by ...* .

Clients want to know, and to recognise clearly, that you are acting on their behalf and that what you say has their interests in mind; your opinion in isolation they can do without. You will find a conscious line of avoiding egocentric-sounding phraseology gives the client the best impression, and helps position you as a professional.

(ix) *Be loyal to your company*

You will win business more easily if your clients have not only a good relationship with you, but also a good image of the organisation you represent. Many firms spend a great deal of money creating a good background image through public relations, design and other techniques. It is easy to undo this good work in a moment.

Consider someone faced with a complaint from a major client because of a missed deadline. It is not the individual's fault, the timing was clear, but a mistake has been made in another department and the client, relying on the arrangement, is understandably upset. People are concerned to protect their personal image and reputation and we can imagine someone saying something along the lines of: *You will appreciate it was out of my hands, I don't know how many times I have told those people how important it is to meet clients' agreed deadlines, but they still seem to have got it wrong.* If they complete the sentence with the word again the damage is made worse and, in either case, the client is left feeling that however good their contact, the organisation behind them is less than efficient. What may have been intended to bolster their image ends up doing the reverse.

You may need to support company policy (even when you disapprove of it), defend colleagues who are less efficient than yourself and positively work at building the image of the whole company. Clients understand that no organisation is perfect, but one that seems to hold itself in low regard is seen as dubious — *"If that is all they think of themselves"* the client thinks, *"how can I have confidence in what they will do for me?"*. It is easy to let the wrong description slip through, and if it becomes a habit, then the damage may be considerable. Boost the image of the whole of the organisation at every opportunity, even when you have to sort out difficulties, it can smooth the path for what follows and make what you do in selling a little more certain.

Offer more

The advice in this book consists of matters you have the power to implement. So let me admit at once that on this point some readers may be dependent on company policy; yet it is an important and powerful aid to increasing sales, so deserves a mention. You can increase the likelihood of success by offering more: more than usual, more than competition, more than expected. Not only in terms of service — that point is made elsewhere — but also in terms of tangible things. Many of the ways that spring to mind are temporary (they have less impact once they are permanent and taken for granted) and might be best described as promotional. For example, offer:

- A free sample or trial (for example, a limited amount of investigatory or design work).
- A free element of product (such as a free survey meeting).
- A limited or exclusive offer.
- A saving, avoiding a coming price increase or an additional one-off discount.

- A higher specification for the cost of the basic offering.
- An incentive (a gift, a trip, a competition).
- Trade-in allowances for upgrading what is bought.
- Better-than-usual credit terms.
- Special guarantees.
- Discounts linked to future purchase.

Intangible factors may be involved here too. For instance, people: a professional firm might promise to, *put John in as project chief, he worked with you successfully previously*. A client might not doubt the competencies of others but still prefer to work with someone they know and trust. Although these are by no means applicable or appropriate to every firm, any of these and more can act to increase sales success. Such devices act in a number of different ways, they:

- Help you achieve a hearing, perhaps for the first time.
- Help improve the weight of the case you can present.
- Can pull commitment forward, persuading people to order now rather than later.
- Can increase the size of an order.
- Can affect the frequency of ordering.

They can also have negative effects, reducing the seeming importance of other benefits; or encouraging clients to shop around, and only buy in turn from whoever are currently offering the best deal. They have to form an organised, integrated part of your company marketing strategy as they can affect image and profitability and cash flow. Some you may control, others you may find suggested and made available by management, perhaps on a temporary basis. Some you may feel would work well and suit your kind of client, in which case you may want to suggest them to management. Such schemes are undeniably useful, but you should never rely on them to the exclusion of making a sound case for buying in other ways.

Overall, there is plenty to think about here (hence the long chapter). Furthermore, even if you get all this right, there can be other problems. The following chapter looks at the perennial topic of handling client objections.

Responding to Clients' Objections

Objections are an inherent part of selling anything. They spring directly from the way clients look at each situation and, whatever the aspect of property with which you deal, you can be sure there will always be some. When people raise them it is not necessarily a sign that there is any problem, indeed it can be a positive sign of some interest on their part. So handling objections is an inherent part of the sales process. If this part is done well it not only redress the balance, or remove the objection entirely, but its being well handled will be impressive. Clients like dealing with people who, as they might put it: *"know their stuff"*. The smooth handling of objections is taken as a sign of professionalism. Not that you will always be able to remove them, there is no merit in trying to persuade your clients that black is white, and the last thing you want is an argument. Rebalancing is what counts as the points in this chapter describe.

Taking the positive view

Some say objections are a sign of interest. This makes perfect sense; clients will hardly bother quizzing you about the details and explanations of something that holds no interests for them. Certainly you should expect to receive them. As we have seen, the way clients go about making buying decisions is to weigh up the pros and cons. They expect to find some things on the downside (few things we buy are perfect, we may be suspicious if it is!). You should watch, however, for the amount of objections you receive. Too many can be a sign that it is your fault. By this I mean that, with experience, you will know roughly how much objection will be raised in a given situation and, to some extent, what issues are likely to be involved. If you find that a client in a meeting you run regularly is raising more objections than you expect, then it may be that:

- You have failed to identify needs sufficiently accurately and what you are saying is therefore off target. More questions may correct this.
- You are suggesting solutions or making suggestions too soon. Clients who feel their situation is unique or who expect a tailored recommendation may feel that what you are saying should follow more thought.
- You may (albeit inadvertently) be giving the impression of a set, standard presentation. Clients disbelieve that products can be all things to all people. They want you to relate what you sell to them individually, not simply go through the standard "patter".

In all these cases, observation may spot what is happening and allow you to adjust your approach.

Therefore, objections can help keep you on track, they are a sign of interest and can also be an opportunity to impress clients by the way you deal with things (not that you should encourage objections just so that you can impressively demolish them!). When they do occur however, and they will, there is no reason why you cannot regard them as something routine and something where how you handle them can act to build your credibility as you go along.

Preventing objections

It is often a sound principle that prevention is better than cure. In objection handling, there are two ways in which prevention can help.

The first is in the area of preparation. Few objections should come at you like a bolt from the blue, most of the topics of objection that occur you will know about and have dealt with previously. Specific circumstances create examples: a good estate agent does not take long to realise that people are going to comment on a third bedroom the size of a small cupboard in a "three-bedroomed house". You should have thought through the perennial objections you receive and, although they will often be phrased in different ways and come with different power and emphasis, you should be ready for them and have various ways of handling them in mind. As and when new, or differently phrased, objections do occur, then you need to consider possible answers to these too and add something about them to your repertoire.

Second, there are objections that may typically remain unspoken. This does not mean they are not in clients' minds, some will be and will form part of the balance upon which they will ultimately decide to buy or not. Where experience shows that this is likely to be happening, it may be necessary for you to raise the issue yourself in the conversation in order to deal with it and get it out of the frame. This is best approached head on: *You may have been wondering about ... let me spend a minute explaining how we deal with that ... You have not mentioned ... do you have any questions about that?*. And if you have thought through the answer, or at least the kind of answer necessary, then you can deal with the matter and perhaps also make it seem reasonably inconsequential.

"Sparring" with objections

We do not demolish objections, we are not even always able to overcome them and we certainly do not want objection handling to develop into an argument. Indeed, it is possible to win arguments with clients — yet lose the chance of business. If, when the client raises an objection, your hackles immediately rise and your every response chips in starting with the words, *Ah, but ...* , there is every chance that the conversation will become confrontational. It is for this reason that you should use the technique known as "sparring". Sparring concerns offering an appropriate initial response, and is useful preliminary to the process of objection handling. The sparring needs to make it clear that you:

- Are listening carefully.
- Will initiate no argument.
- Accept the point made and will deal with it rather than deny it.
- Will treat it seriously.
- Do not think the client is being contentious, or unnecessarily demanding.

If you say something that positions how you will deal with the objection: *That's a good point Mr Client, I can see I must give you more information in that area ...* , *You are quite right to raise that, it is an important point, let me ...* , preferably something that includes at least a hint of agreement, then you will provoke feelings in the client's mind that will make dealing with the objection easier. With the client saying to themselves: *Good, there's not going to be an argument* or *They accept the point, let's see what they say about it* then they will be more receptive to what you say next. This principle may be more important than it seems because some objection areas are difficult and can quickly become emotional. Sparring has the effect of "lowering the temperature" of the conversation prior to providing the answer.

There is another important result of using this technique. Sometimes you will get objections that are new, that you are not expecting, not familiar with or that, if only for a moment, throw you. These can present real difficulty when you feel you have to come back fast with a credible response and leave no hiatus in the conversation. Luckily, the construction of the human mind is such that in the time it will take you to say something like: *That's a good point, Mr Client, we are certainly going to have to satisfy you that we can meet your needs in that area. Let me ...* , then your mind can be doing a great deal of thinking and you may well be on the way to an answer. Sparring builds in some thinking time just when you may need it most. It sets up a situation that is as favourable as possible to dealing with the objection itself, and makes it more likely that you can do so effectively.

Providing an answer

Never attempt to deal with an objection until you have sufficient information. If you assume wrongly exactly what is meant or treat a serious point superficially you will be in trouble and make matters worse. Objections must not be allowed to put you on the defensive. Sparring helps set the scene. Two other initial responses are also worth bearing in mind.

First, never be afraid to respond to a question with a question of your own. This will be understood and accepted, after all how can you be expected to comment sensibly about a point until you know exactly what lies behind it? More than one question may be quite acceptable, although you should make it clear what you are doing: *"That's a fair point, Mr Client, let me make sure I understand exactly what you mean, can you tell me ..."*. This is an important point as simple questions or comments may either disguise a deeper point or, more often, can have several possible interpretations. Consider an example. A client comments on price (they so often do!) saying something like: *"That is very expensive"*. What do they mean? It is a comment, not even phrased as a question and could mean many things, for instance:

- "It is more than I expected."
- "It is more than I pay now."
- "It is more than another quote."
- "It is over my budget."
- "That cost is beyond my authority to decide."
- "I'm not convinced it is value for money."
- "Will you negotiate?"
- "I'm not clear what I get for it."
- "It is a lot to pay at once."
- "I don't understand."
- "No."
- "Can the specification be reduced to cut costs?"
- "I will have to think about that."
- "I cannot decide now."

You may be able to think of, or have experienced, more such meanings. Many of these interpretations need answering along different lines; it makes the point clearly that you have to understand exactly what is meant before you deal with it.

Second, if something is thrown out as a comment or challenge, such as, *But that is very expensive* in the above example, in a form that is not a question, then it may be turned back to the client as a question to clarify. Thus: But that is very expensive could be followed by the question: *Yes, Mr Client, it is a considerable cost, though I would suggest, of course, it is a good investment, but what exactly are you saying? Is it more than you had budgeted for?*. This kind of approach does a number of things quickly:

- It acknowledges the point (there is no merit in denying it is a great deal of money if the client clearly feels that it is).
- Suggests you will be happy to discuss it.
- Makes asking for more information about their concern seem helpful.

Once these preliminaries are out of the way, you can move on to addressing the objection. If you continue to keep in mind the image of a balance (described earlier) and bear in mind that there will be points of varying importance and weight, on either side, then the job is one of ordering the balance, or reordering the one you have described, so that it presents a favourable basis for a positive decision. Often clients are not going to automatically buy if the balance is positive, they are only going to buy from you if your described balance stacks up better than those of any competitors that they may also be evaluating.

You have only four options that you can use in rebalancing, so at least mechanistically there is no great complication here. These are to:

- Persuade people that their objection is false, in other words, it exerts no weight on the minus side of the balance.
- Concede that they have a point, but explain that the effect on the balance is minimal, reducing the weight they saw it exerting.
- Concede completely and in this case — and the others — combine within your answer a re-emphasis on the plus points, that is the benefits.
- And, occasionally, something raised as a negative point can be shown actually to be a positive.

Careful description of price will minimise the incidence of price objections, careful handling of them will remove what can often be a major obstacle to agreement; this is worth a separate word.

Handling price

Of all the things that come up as objections this is often the most frequent and the most difficult. Of course, all clients want value for money and, in many areas, they will negotiate if they can (negotiation is an additional skill and body of techniques to that of selling, beyond the scope of this book, although I have written on this in *Successful Negotiating* [How to Books]). At the least clients want to assess value for money and often to compare what you offer in this respect with competition. So how do you handle this? First, the way you position price has an effect on the likelihood of your subsequently receiving price objections. Price should rarely be dealt with in isolation, by describing it alongside benefits then you make it speak much more of value for money.

Beware also of presenting price so that it runs foul of the way in which people regard money psychologically. For example:

- *Avoid price barriers*: We all see goods priced at £9.99 in retail outlets, and somehow this is perceived as being significantly less than something at £10. Similarly with higher amounts, £4995 seems less than £5000, a house priced at £199,500 is set below the nearest round figure (and tax thresholds complicate this). This seems silly to many, we *know* it is virtually the same thing, but there is a great deal of research to back up the psychological response to such things — the lower price really does mean agreement to buy is more likely. I suggest you do not worry about why, but use the fact where you can.

- *Amortise price*: This is the technique of quoting a figure of, say, £1000 (or around a thousand) per month, which seems less than £12,000 over a year. This can be used in a variety of ways to split larger sums down, spreading them over different budgets, people, or time frames. Additionally, any way of stressing the economies of scale is also part of this.

If you have more flexibility in setting prices, as is the case with those selling a tailored service, for example, then:

- *Judge price range carefully*: To say it will be between £4000 and £7000 may seem too vague, whereas £4000–5000 or even £5500 may be acceptable as a first ballpark figure. A second point here, always be careful about the top point of the range. Quote something you then exceed and the client's perception of you changes for the worse and does so fast: *"These people always go over their estimate"* — come in below estimate and it helps ensure they come back to you next time.
- *Avoid round figures*: When quoting bespoke arrangements, as is often the case with consultancy and fees, with the work based on the client's unique brief, it will not be credible if it comes to a round figure like £10,000. If it does, people will assume that this is an impossible coincidence and probably assume also that you have worked out a figure and then rounded it up.

Finally here, a useful way to remember some good phraseology when dealing with price can be hung round the four mathematical symbols:

+   mention: this *plus* ... / *in addition to* ...
−   mention: ...*reducing* costs / *eliminating* the need for ... / *lessening* this ... / *minimise* ...
×   mention: ... something producing *multiple* advantages or opportunities / *enhanced* service / ...*greater* productivity / *more* satisfaction

÷   mention: *amortise* costs over .../*spread* across .../*divided* between .../*apportioned* to ...

This is simply a mechanism to prompt you towards the right kind of language.

Dealing with the ups and downs of price

Price is always an issue and when it changes this can focus more attention on it. Usually the problem of changes is with increases, but sometimes there are, curiously, also problems with reductions in price. We will review reduction first. Sometimes the company can reduce price (not by negotiating, but as a marketing tactic), which may be linked to various things, including competitive pressure. Unsolicited gifts can arouse suspicion, and if clients are told *"Prices are down by 10%"*, their first reaction may not be *"Good"*, but rather *"Why?"*.

Reactions include:

- *Replacement*: It is assumed that a product line is being discontinued, that it has become obsolete and will be replaced by something better or more up to date. Here reasons are vital, you need to offer reassurance of quality and say what makes the reduction possible.
- *Trouble*: It is assumed that the company is in trouble, usually financial trouble, and that a rapid cut is designed to produce cash that will assist the recovery process. Here you need to boost their overall image of the company, talk about long-term plans and make it clear that business is going well. Clearly nothing like this is compatible with the professional image many readers will be trying to cultivate.
- *Low quality*: Clients assume that what is under offer is of low quality and perhaps different from the rest of the range or from what they are used to receiving from you. Mention quality control, tests and checks. Tell them the reasons and reassure them regarding the specific offer. With one-off things — an individual house reduced in price, for example — the first thought prompted can be that there must be something wrong with it, *If no one else wants it, why should I?*.
- *Further savings*: a cut may be taken, perhaps in conjunction with one of the other factors, to mean greater cuts are to follow. This can

also result in delay — *I'll confirm later* — and you need to make it clear if this is not the case. If the cut is for a short time this can be quoted, if there are regular dates for future change remind people of this too.

On the other hand, and maybe with greater regularity, prices may be increased and you need to discuss this with clients who regard it as unreasonable. In this case:

- *Explain the reasons*: and there should be reasons! Cost increases, economic situations — better still link it to the client's own situation, when did they last raise prices and why?
- *Help them reduce the impact*: this can be done by suggesting placing larger orders (if quantity rates apply); early ordering (even one more order at the old price may soften the blow); suggest ways to save associated costs (for example, reducing expenses or time taken in consulting work).

All those dealing with you understand that what you do costs money and that prices change. Make the explanation clear and whatever the change you can keep the client on your side, continue to retain his business and even sell more than before.

A last word on this: perhaps more than anywhere else, price objections, in all their manifestations, are things for which you must be ready. Prepare well and deal with them with authority and confidence and you will find you can handle them.

Do not knock competition

Sometimes you will be asked outright about competition: *What about firm X?* or: *We also plan to talk to company Y, do you know them?*. Two responses are to be avoided:

- Do not single them out: *Yes, I know them, they are my biggest competitor*. Such a response is likely to make the client think he should check them out, indeed you may end up with one more active competitor vying for the business.
- Do not knock them: *I certainly do know them, I thought everyone knew the trouble they are having in the market at present*. It is just life that at that point they declare that they have done business together very

satisfactorily in the past, or that there is some other connection that makes such a knock particularly inappropriate. Besides, it is difficult not to let such comments sound like sour grapes.

You need a more constructive response, such as: *There are a dozen or more competitors for us in this sector, we come across them all and each has certain strengths.* This makes checking them all out seem complicated, and while giving no detail, does acknowledge that you know they are also good. This is also a more credible response.

Another, perhaps similar, thing that can happen is that clients refer to the competition's comments about you: *Your competitors tell me you are having staff problems currently and difficulty in getting things done on time.* This kind of comment can be turned round: *If my rivals are making a point of saying that kind of thing, then my first reaction is only to be pleased. It seems to me to indicate we have them worried in some way — we are certainly busy, and recruiting more people, but we are on top of things and you will find nothing to complain about with regard to service.*

Care in all references to competition always pays off, the last thing you want is a protracted argument, prompted by some detailed negative comment you make, the client may then feel they must defend their position as accepting it may make their past decision to deal with another firm look ill-judged. One last point, if a competitor is named (and it is something you can do worse than ask about if it is not), then information about what you are up against may help you decide on the line you will take with the client; provided you know something about your competitor's strengths and weaknesses that is.

Avoid untenable comparisons

There is an old saying to the effect that while you can compare apples with apples, there is no merit in comparing apples with old shoes. Yet clients do the latter all the time. They say something like: *That's all very well but I can get the same thing from firm X on much better terms.* What they actually mean is that they can purchase something *rather different* from elsewhere. On that basis they are no doubt correct, there are always many permutations on offer in any particular industry. They seek justification of your package, and often of your price (they may want a discount), in comparison with the quoted alternative — although they rarely elaborate on the details of that other offering.

The answer here cannot lie with a direct comparison when, as is most often the case, the two things are not exactly the same. A quoted competitor may be less costly, but the specification may be less, the quality lower, less may be included, associated costs may be higher, credit terms or guarantees may be different, design details may vary, and delivery or timing may be longer or less certain. The possibilities are many.

A sales-orientated response must identify and then deal with these differences. The first answer may well be, *Yes, you can get something similar elsewhere* (do not deny it, that way lies fruitless argument) *but it is certainly not identical, in our discussions you have emphasised the need for reliability, our* ... and back to the benefits you have identified they want. In some circumstances, your first response may need to be a question; you have to find out more about what is being offered to discover how it differs from your offering. In terms of price, if yours are more expensive then the additional amount over and above your competitor can only be explained and justified by reference to the gap between what the two parties offer, in other words, what does the extra amount of money buy? Does it provide better service, higher quality or what? Or what would paying less lead them to miss? — you can discuss it both ways round.

Clients certainly want value for money, they also want a "good deal", but they will not sacrifice key requirements for savings that may prove a false economy. It is a fact that many of the most successful products and services in many markets are not the cheapest. Cost and quality go together and you should sell your quality with confidence. In this field this is particularly so: who wants their dream home designed by a second-rate architect, or a house surveyed by a surveyor of dubious skill and experience? Avoid odious comparisons that clients may make only to antagonise, or as an opening to negotiation, and make sure that whatever the client may do, you only compare apples with apples.

Use the "boomerang" technique

Something else that can be useful in handling objections is a particular form of words, which turns an objection back on itself so that the question posed links to the answer. Thus:

Buyer: "As you know this is now very urgent, I don't know that we have time for elaborate surveys."

Seller: "It is because I know you want things sorted out fast, Mr Client, that I am suggesting the survey. It will not take long and could avoid more significant delays if you went ahead without it and hit any snags."

If the question is linked to something that the client rates highly, and if they need something urgently, then this can make a case for the line you present. It is a manner of presentation that can make the client feel that his key issue is genuinely being acknowledged, and that the answer is being dealt with in a way that addresses it.

Saving face

Sometimes clients' objections prove false. This makes them challenge some point when actually the facts are entirely on their side and the balance is good and positive. The temptation in a hectic meeting, especially one in which a number of objections have been raised, including perhaps some difficult ones, is heave a sigh of relief that one is mistaken and blurt out the equivalent of *"You're wrong!"*. This is a natural reaction but can result in the client being made to feel bad, or worse, feeling he has been made to look silly. This is something to be avoided if good relations are to be maintained.

There can be many reasons for the client making a mistake, an original impression about the company and what it does may be wrong: out of date perhaps. They may have misheard something or misinterpreted something they read, or it could be your fault — you may have phrased something badly, not gone into sufficient detail, continued talking while their attention was elsewhere; or you may not know where the fault lies, indeed it may not matter.

What is important here is to let the client down lightly. Suggest that it is an easy or commonly made mistake. This may still leave them feeling bad. It may be better to suggest you are at fault, albeit in a general and unspecified way: *Sorry, perhaps I gave you the wrong impression about that, the fact is ... , If I was insufficiently clear about that, I apologise, it is not, in fact, a problem; the fact is ...* . This works well in either case. Sometimes clients know they are at fault and prefer an approach that avoids laying blame or making them feel bad about it. Sometimes it is no one's fault, but the approach is still seen to be sensitive. A little care in this area can get over what otherwise can be small upsets to the smooth progress of the meeting and the development of a positive case. You should not overdo it, or it will risk sounding patronising, but do avoid drawing attention to errors.

This whole area — the smooth, assured handling of clients' objections — is an important one to get to grips with. Not least it avoids there being any hiatus between the presentation of a strong case and the next stage, now reviewed in chapter 10, obtaining a commitment or "closing to get agreement to buy".

Gaining a Commitment 10

It is perhaps the need to close (the jargon word for completing the sales process to secure agreement) that sets selling — persuasive communication — apart from other more straightforward kinds of communication, and it can involve getting the other person to make a decision, change their minds or even upturn the habits of a lifetime. As such, it can present problems. It is psychologically difficult in some senses for whoever is doing the selling, holding out as it does the prospect of success, or failure and lack of agreement. Furthermore, clients sometimes find it difficult to make a decision. It is a stage that is dependent on what has gone before, but it is also one that must occur. If you cannot or will not close and handle that stage, then your sales effectiveness will always be less effective than it might otherwise be. Here we review this crucial stage.

Your own commitment to close

Closing a deal is the ultimate objective of all selling. You can reach it in stages, in which case you have to close, a number of times, on all the interim commitments of which there can be many, it may represent a close to get a client to say:

- Yes, I'll see you.
- Yes, send something (a brochure or other literature).
- Yes, let me have a quotation in writing (or a proposal).
- Yes, let's meet again to take things further.
- Yes, I'll buy it (the ultimate decision).

Closing is less a stage of the sales process, than just a phrase or, more often, a question. You have to know when to close and you have to actually do it. Closing is often a weak area of selling (especially for those who are professionals first and sales people only as an adjunct to that), although that may be less because it is done badly, than because it is not done at all. Most people, understandably disliking it when people say *No* (and not all prospects say no politely), may find themselves taking a safer route to ending the meeting. They say things like: *I hope this has been useful — I hope I have been able to give you all the details you need at this stage — Is there anything else I can add before we finish?*. This kind of non-close finish almost guarantees a pleasant end to the meeting, with clients responding with statements such as: *That's been very useful, thanks very much for coming to see me — You've given me all the information I need at this stage, thank you very much for your time.* Everyone likes to feel they have been helpful and receive thanks; but such responses are usually followed by two other little words: *Good bye*, drawing the meeting to a close before a commitment has been made and any follow-up action can be arranged.

So resolve to close. You have to be thick-skinned about the rejection; I do not know an area of the property world with a one hundred per cent strike rate, so there is always some. But if you aim to close every time at every stage then, along with a little rejection, you may well receive more business than any of your more faint-hearted competitors (or colleagues!).

Watch for "buying signals"

The advice that is often given is that the best time to close is at the earliest time possible. This is a little glib, but there is some truth in it, to the extent that you can leave things too late and the moment passes. Certainly you need to watch for signs that the prospect is ready to make a decision. Left alone some people are indecisive, or at the very least they will take a long time to make up their minds. This may be for constructive reasons — you must be wary of trying to shortcut the weighing up factors, which they see as making a decision possible — but if it is out of what some might see as a perverse desire to delay, then closing may act as a catalyst to prompt a decision.

Remember closing does not cause people to buy, only the power of persuasion from the picture you have built up and the case you have presented can do that — by creating the interest that closing then converts into becoming a decision to buy. So the final kind of feedback you need during a sales meeting is in the form of what are called "buying signals".

These are less easy to define than to spot. Some will be in the form of a series of signs of interest, expressions, comments, noises even, nods certainly, all of which indicate satisfaction with what is being presented. The most tangible sign is probably comments about the situation that will pertain after purchase, for example: *Then, after we have (done this), we can ... — Once this stage is out of the way, we ...* . Such comments may be interspersed with questions and other signs that some portion of the decision is still to be made, finally the questions may only be for reassurance; in the buyer's own mind they have made the decision and closing can confirm it out in the open.

You will come to trust your judgment in this area and it is worthwhile noting what signals you feel you see, and whether they provide an accurate indication of how things went from there on, as guide for the future.

Obtaining feedback from a "trial close"

It is important to realise that closing is not a one-shot situation, some client encounters involve a number of closes: with, for instance, the first rejected but the last agreed. One early close that may be used to obtain feedback — often with no real hope of closing at the point it is used — is the so-called "trial close". This can be any kind of close in terms of technique: you may be fairly sure the answer will be a no, but the way it is phrased can be designed to give valuable clues as to how close you are getting to acceptance or on what element you should now concentrate to complete the process. For example, if you attempt to close, the client might say: *Now wait a minute, we still need to discuss X*, and you move on to discuss just that. This is a useful technique and provides an alternative way of obtaining very focused feedback.

How to close

Closing is not a stage but more a simple question or comment. All you need is a particular choice of phraseology to match the client and the circumstances. There are many permutations, but the most often used are perhaps the following:

Direct request

For example, *Shall we go ahead with the survey then, so that you can move onto the next stage soon?*

Requests such as this should be used where the client prefers to make their own decisions.

Command

This effectively says: *Do this, perhaps linking it to what logically follows: With that done you can ... .*

This can be used where the client:

* has difficulty in making a decision; or
* has considerable respect for the sales person.

Immediate gain

For example, *You mentioned that this year the company really needs to improve productivity. If you can give me the go-ahead today, I can make sure that you see specific results within three months' time.*

This could be used where, by acting fast, the client can receive an important benefit, whereas delay might cause certain or severe problems. The "hard" version of this is the fear close (below).

Fear close

As in something like: *Unless you can give me the go-ahead now, then I am afraid ...* followed by stating the penalties of delay. This is a more powerfully phrased version of "immediate gain", and should be used with discretion.

Alternatives

For example, *Both these approaches meet your criteria. Which one do you prefer to implement?* And definitely not, as a delegate once suggested to me on a course: *Are you going to buy from me or firm X?*.

This could be used where you are happy to obtain a commitment on any one of the possible alternatives.

Best solution

For example, *You want work done within your budget, so that it matches the rest of the building and so that life is not disrupted during the time work is being done. The best fit with all these requirements is "X". When's the best time to start?*

This should be used when the client has a mix of needs, some of which can be better met by the competition, but which, when taken as a whole, are best met by your solution.

Question or objection

For example, *If we can make that revision, can you get the finance director to agree to proceed?*.

This should be used where you know you can answer the client's objection to his satisfaction.

Assumption

For example, *Fine. I've got all the information I need to meet your requirements. Once I get back to the office, I'll prepare the necessary paperwork and you'll have matters in hand by the end of the month.*

In other words, we assume the client has said Yes and continue the conversation on this basis.

Concession

Trade only a small concession to obtain agreement now or agree to proceed only on stage one.

However you phrase things, and whatever kind of close you use, the key thing here is to actually close and do so firmly; more than once if necessary and with every client at every stage of the process.

"Let me think about it"

Clients may say a number of things other than "Yes" or "No", and many people find the most difficult to deal with is that little phrase, *Let me think about it.* This is essentially positive, yet if you just walk away from it — allowing them to do just that — then you may never speak to that client again. Some clients who say this do actually mean, No. But you need to know whether to take it at face value or not. So what is the best response? It is often difficult to think of a reason why the client should *not* think about it (unless you can contribute pressing reasons to decide at once). So the best route may be to agree: and not simply to agree but to urge the client to think about it. Tell them it is an important decision, tell them they must not make it lightly, tell them they should not be rushed, that they must be certain; however you phrase it make sure you are clearly on the side of thinking about it. But then ask why exactly they still need to think about it, or what elements of the decision still need review. Often something is then volunteered here: there is a particular sticking point, something about the case has been less well made than the rest, or there is some area where more information seems to be needed. Then you can try turning the intention back to more discussion:

Client: "Let me think about it."
Property professional: "Of course, it's a big decision, you have to be sure."
Client: "That's right."
Property professional: "You must be sure it's right in every respect, is there any particular aspect which you need to think about?"
Client: "Well, I suppose it's the timescale that worries me most, it would be bound to affect current work."
Property professional: "To some extent yes, but we can minimise that, perhaps I did not explain how we would approach that sufficiently; can I go over it again before we finish?"
Client: "OK. I want to have it all clear in my mind."

Then the meeting is under way again and there is no reason why it cannot move on towards another close, which is agreed without any more wish to think about it. The phrase is regularly a sign that something (or several somethings) — in which case you may be able to get the client to list them before you suggest more discussion — is still unclear or unresolved.

There is an alternative here, however. The client may ask for time to think about it not because they need time to think, but for another reason. Perhaps the two most likely are the need to confer with someone else in the organisation (the real decision maker), or maybe there is a meeting planned with a competitor for comparative purposes. In this case, careful questioning may discover either possibility, or others. Then the action on which you plan to close may change; maybe the first step is to try to organise a meeting with their colleague (sometimes they appreciate help with any internal selling that may be necessary), or to ensure you get a further hearing after the competitor meeting.

Again, we see that the more the information you find out at every stage, the better position you are in to take things further. Such techniques are not infallible, but if they increase your strike rate even a little they are well worth pursuing, and you may be surprised by how often *Let me think about it* leads not to thinking about it, but to extended discussion and a — positive — decision.

When they say *Yes*

Let us assume you are going to achieve a good strike rate — think positive! — and some of the people you meet with will agree to buy. Then what? Well, the first thing is to thank them, you do not need to grovel, but the nature of the relationship makes a thank you highly appropriate. It is good practice to couple the thanks with reassurance: *Thanks very much, Mr Client, I am sure you will find all this works out well.* Then consider any practical points that need to be dealt with at this stage:

- Is there documentation to be completed (guarantee, contract, service arrangement etc)?
- Do you need a signature?
- Is there information you need (invoice address, order number, delivery arrangements etc)?
- Are there points still to be discussed/agreed (delivery date)?

All such matters must be dealt with in a prompt and business-like way, you are still on show and it is still possible for the client to change their mind, or demand to negotiate more on price — something that could negate the result you think you have achieved. So deal with such things promptly and end the meeting. Do not chatter on in a fit of euphoria: many a person has talked themselves out of an order again at this stage. Of course, some social chat may be important; there are deals where both parties regard lunch afterwards as natural. Be sure the client — who no doubt values his time highly — really wants to extend the contact. And decide the objectives of such an extended meeting (it is surely part of or the start of a working relationship). Do you drop business, talk no "shop" and treat it socially, or use it to move on to other topics? It is important to meet the client's needs in this respect. He will not like it if he planned to use the time constructively and you only talk of golf or vice versa.

Once you have left the client, never fail to double-check your internal paperwork is completed. People have been known to forget something vital — a figure or other detail — after a good lunch!

When you have obtained agreement, then the sales process may be at an end (although it may be the beginning of ongoing sales activity to hold and develop the business). But there is more to bear in mind: first, what happens when things have to be put in writing, and then a final section before we summarise adds some thoughts to what has been covered so far.

Writing Persuasive Proposals

Having gone through the sequence of a typical meeting in some detail over the past few chapters, we must accept here that it is not always possible to get to a conclusion in one meeting; there may be another necessary and unavoidable stage, one that is certainly particularly relevant for those selling bespoke services. While not every property business requires it, when it is necessary written persuasion must be as good as that spoken face to face; and yet it is often weaker. At any stage of checking you out, the client has the right to say No. Everything you do — responding to an enquiry, holding an initial meeting and so on — has a cumulative effect. It is, when completed satisfactorily, a step further on towards obtaining a decision. Written proposals are often a key part of the sequence of events. A good one takes things on down the sequence, while a bad one may stop progress dead in its tracks.

Actually it is worse than that. A proposal that is only inadequate in some detail compared with one from a competitor (and often your proposal is in competition) may be placed second. Your proposal may be rated less impressive or appropriate by only a whisker — but you are still out. So the quality of written proposals is vital.

Proposals may vary. Some projects may be booked after sending a page or two of text by e-mail (as was writing this book come to think of it; sorry I digress), others may need substantial documents as part of the process of confirming a project. Whatever is necessary it must be done right.

If putting things in writing is not your stock in trade to the same extent as other aspects of your communication, then maybe it is something you need to beef up. To be productive and successful you need the ability to decide what to say, to get words down in the right style and to do so quickly. You need to create powerful documents that inform, perhaps clarifying complex issues, that persuade — and that impress.

In your mind's eye ...

As a small digression, I cannot resist referring to the Video Arts training film *The Proposal* (which I highly recommend).

The film shows someone struggling to complete a sales proposal. He day-dreams of the rapturous reception with which the buyer will greet the arrival of his deathless prose and the certainty of an order to follow. But a voice interrupts — *but it's not like that is it?* and his vision changes to a less rosy image. This time when a secretary comes into the office to deliver his proposal, we see the buyer (John Cleese) sitting at his desk, a picture of hung-over misery. He is slowly dropping Alka-Seltzer tablets into a glass and physically wincing at the fizzing noise they make.

There can be few better images to have in mind when you sit down to write a proposal. If you aim to make your next one combat that sort of barrier, you will have to think carefully about it and invest it with some power.

First, let us define terms.

Quotations versus proposals

It may be worth being clear about what exactly is meant by the two words "proposal" and "quotation". Although they are sometimes used in a way that appears similar, in sales terms they each imply something very different.

Proposals have to describe, explain and justify what they suggest. They normally make recommendations (often bespoke ones), and they should assume that their job is to persuade.

On the other hand, a quotation is normally a much simpler document. They simply set out a particular — usually requested — option. They say that something is available and what it costs. They assume, rightly or wrongly, that the sales job is done and that persuasion is unnecessary. This may be true, especially with repeat assignments/work. But many quotations should have more, sometimes much more, of the proposal about them. Here the review is concerned with the more complex proposals, though the principles concerned might also act to beef up any quotations you use.

Choice of format

There are two main overall approaches to the format of proposals. Sometimes a letter, albeit maybe a longish one, is entirely appropriate. Indeed, doing more than this can overstate a case and put the recipient off. It is seen as over-engineering, and as increasing costs. Alternatively, what is necessary is much more like a report, although one with a persuasive bent.

Note: Discussion document: This is a document for a stage before a proposal is appropriate, classically, this sets the scene for a meeting, dealing with background and defining areas and ideas to be discussed at a meeting. As with all such documentation exactly how it is written is vital to its success. A subsequent proposal is thus an extension of this when both are involved.

Consider both levels of formality in turn, and when and why each may be appropriate.

Letter proposals

This is what the name suggests. It starts with a first sheet set out like a letter, which begins *Dear ...* . It may be several pages long, with a number of subheadings, but it is essentially less formal than a report-style proposal. This style is appropriate when:

- A more detailed proposal is not needed because there would be insufficient content, or an over formality.
- The objective (or request) is only to summarise discussions that have taken place.
- There are no outstanding issues (unsolved at prior meetings, for instance).
- There is no threat of competition.

Where these, or some of them, do not apply another approach is necessary.

Formal proposal

This is a report-style document, usually bound in some way and thus more elaborate and formal. Such a proposal is appropriate when:

- Recommendations are complex.
- What is being sold is high in cost (or, just as important, will be seen as being so).
- There is more than one "client": a committee, a recommender and decision maker acting together or some other combination of people who need to confer and will thus see exactly the same thing.
- (Linked to the previous point) you have not met some of those who will be instrumental in making the decision.
- You know you have competition and are being compared.

I am often asked: *How many copies of a proposal should I send?*.

The short answer is to ask the client and send as many as are requested. In many businesses it is common for there to be multiple decision makers or influencers. Where this is even suspected it is doubly-wise to ask how many copies of a proposal will be required. If you have seen, say, two people and the answer is three copies, maybe there is someone else you need to be aware of and more questions (or even another meeting) become the order of the day before you move on. One way or another, you have to find out the role the new person plays and make sure that the proposal addresses them as well as others.

In anything to do with selling, the client and their views rank high. What they want should rightly influence the kind of proposal you put in. Ask them questions such as:

- How formal should it be?
- What sort of detail is expected?
- How long should it be?
- How many people will see it? (As mentioned above.)
- When do they want to receive it?

You do not have to follow their answers slavishly, but must make a considered judgment. For example, if you are dealing with someone you know, they may suggest not being too formal. But, if you know you have competition and they are in discussion with other potential suppliers, it may still pay to set out something more formal than a letter; after all, your document and someone else's will be compared alongside each other. In a comparison between a letter-style and more formal proposal, the former tends to look weaker, especially when related to value for money.

Timing

Timing is worth a particular word. It is important to meet clients' deadlines, even if, in some cases, it means "burning the midnight oil". However, it is likely that people want your proposal to reflect your *considered* opinion. Promising that on a complex matter *"in 24 hours"* may simply not be credible. Too much speed in such a case can cast doubts on quality and originality. This is especially true for those in a consultative or advisory role, and when solutions are positioned as being truly bespoke. In consequence, it may occasionally be politic to delay something, asking for more time than you actually need to enhance the feeling of tailoring and consideration when it arrives.

At this stage you know something about the client's needs, you know who is involved in the decision (ie those who will read whatever you write) and when the proposal is required. Remember the need for preparation: add in any time that com- posing such a document demands you spend with colleagues — in discussion, brainstorming — and set aside sufficient time to do a good writing job.

Once something has been posted, then you have live with it. You cannot reasonably telephone a correction later or send a "revised page 7" to be slotted in by the prospect. With all that in mind, let us turn to see how the content should be arranged and dealt with in a proposal.

Proposal content and arrangement

While the form and content of a proposal can vary, the main divisions are best described as:

- The introduction (often preceded by a contents page).
- The statement of need.
- The recommendations (or solution).
- Costs.
- Areas of detail (such as timing, logistics, staffing and technical specification).

- Closing statement (or summary).
- Additional information (of prime or lesser importance in the form of appendices).

Each section may need a number of subheadings and their length may vary with context but they form a convenient way of reviewing the key issues about the construction of a proposal and are thus commented on in turn:

Title/contents page

A proposal of any complexity needs the equivalent of a book's title page. This states whom, or which organisation, it is for, what it is about and whom it is from. This page can also give the contact details of the proposer (which, if not here, must be somewhere within the proposal) and some people like to feature the logo of the recipient organisation on it, as well as their own.

This should be followed by a front sheet on which the contents of the proposal are listed and which gives the page numbers. It may make it look more interesting if there are subheadings as well as main headings, especially if the main headings are bland, for instance *"The introduction"*. Better still, make sure the headings are not bland.

Note: The headings that follow are descriptive of the functions and role of the sections, and not recommendations for headings you should necessarily use.

Introduction

Remember that a proposal is a sales document. As such, the opening must command attention, establish interest and lead into the main text, making people want to read on. As the introduction has to undertake a number of important, yet routine, tasks, ahead of them it may be best to start with a sentence (or more) that is interesting, rings bells with the client and sets the tone for the document.

Thereafter, there are a number of other roles for the introduction, for instance, it may need to:

- Establish the background.
- Refer to past meetings and discussions.
- Recap decisions made to date.

- Quote experience.
- Acknowledge terms of reference.
- List the names of those involved in the discussions and/or preparation of the document.

Think too about how any necessary areas such as complaints procedure are expressed. As none of this is as interesting as what will follow, this section should concentrate on essentials and be kept short. Its final words should act as a bridge to the next section.

Statement of need

This section needs to set out, with total clarity, the brief in terms of the needs of the client, especially those expecting bespoke service. It describes the scope of the requirement, and may act to recap and confirm what was agreed at a prior meeting that the proposal would cover.

It is easy to ask why this section should be necessary. Surely the client knows what they want? Indeed they have perhaps just spent a considerable amount of time telling you exactly that. But this statement is still important.

Its role is to make clear that *you do have complete understanding of the situation*. It emphasises the identity of views between the two parties and gives credibility to your later suggestions by making clear that they are based firmly on the real — and, if appropriate, individual — needs that exist. Without this it might be possible for the client to assume that you are suggesting what is best (or perhaps most profitable) for you; or simply making a standard suggestion when they expect a tailored one.

This section is also of key importance if the proposal is to be seen by people who were not party to the original discussions; for them, it may be the first clear statement of this picture. Again, this part should link naturally into the next section.

Recommendations (or solution)

This is often the longest section and needs to be logically arranged and divided (as do all the sections) to make it manageable. Clear and informative headings are needed. Here you state what approach you feel meets the requirements. This may be:

- Standard, in the sense that it is a list of, for example, recommended approaches that you have discussed and sell as a standard solution.
- "Bespoke", as with the approach a consultant might set out to a project.

In either case, this section needs to be set out in a way that is "benefits-led", spelling out the advantages and making clear what the solution will mean to, or do for, the individual client as well as specifying the technical features. Thus, do not just list what you will do, but state what the result will be or how a stage will move things forward once completed.

Remember, the sales task here is threefold: to explain, to do so persuasively, and to differentiate. Never forget, when putting together a proposal, that you may be in competition and what you present will be compared, often closely, with the offerings of others. A focus on the client's needs is usually the best way to ensure the readers' attention; nothing must be said that does not have clear client relevance.

One further emphasis is particularly important here: individuality. It is easy to store standard documents on disk these days and, indeed, it may be possible to edit one proposal into a new version that does genuinely suit a similar need elsewhere (although double-check that you have changed the client's name and any other individual references!). But, if a proposal is intended to look tailored it must do just that and there must be no hint of it seeming standardised. This is sufficiently important to re-emphasise — bespoke proposals must never seem standard in any sense. A client knows that you must get many similar requests, but will still appreciate clear signs that you have prepared something "tailored just for them".

Only when this section has been covered thoroughly should you move on to refer to costs, because only when the client appreciates exactly what value and benefits are being provided can they consider costs in context.

Costs

Fees and all costs must be stated clearly, and not look disguised (although certain techniques for presenting the figures are useful, for example amortising costs — describing something as costing £1000 per month, rather than £12,000 for the year; describing and costing stages separately).

All the necessary detail must be there, including any items that are:

- options
- extras
- associated expenses.

These must be shown and made clear.

Without going into all the details of marketing and pricing policy, do note that:

- Price should be linked as closely as possible to benefits.
- This section must establish or reinforce that you offer value for money, not just state figures baldly.
- Invoicing details and trading terms often need including, and must always be clear; mistakes here tend to be expensive (in the UK, remember to make clear whether price is inclusive of VAT).
- Overseas, attention must be given to currency considerations.
- Comparisons may need to be made with competition or with past projects.
- Range figures (necessary in some kinds of property business) must be used carefully (do not make the gap too wide and never exceed the upper range figure).
- With some work in the property sector, you may need to refer to tax or legal requirements that increase overall costs.

Look carefully at how you arrange this section; it is not just facts and numbers, it must be as persuasive as any other part of the document.

You may ask: *Won't some people turn straight to the "costs" section?*.

Yes, without a doubt this happens — indeed, it is only realistic to assume that some readers will look at this page or pages before reading *anything* else. Certainly for them, there needs to be sufficient explanation, cost justification and, above all, clear benefits linked in here. Just the bald figures can be very off-putting. This section must not only deal with its discrete topic, but it must act to persuade the reader who starts here that it is worth turning to the front and reading through from the beginning. Write it to achieve just that.

John de Forte and Guy Jones, authors of *Proposals, Pitches and Beauty Parades*, focus primarily on the most complex areas of proposing, those where competitive tendering is the best description of what occurs. Here the presentation of price is perhaps even more important, but their advice is good for any situation:

Treat it (presenting the price) as an opportunity to convey positive messages about your commitment to giving value for money and how you intend to help the client monitor and control costs; try to show that you want the service to be as cost-effective as possible. Apart from giving the fee itself, describe also the basis of charging and, if it is a long-term assignment, how fee levels might be determined in the future or when it would be appropriate to review them. If a detailed fee analysis is required, this may be better dealt with in an appendix.

Areas of detail

There are additional topics that it may be necessary to deal with here, as mentioned above: timing, logistics, staffing etc. At times, these are best combined with costs within one section. Not if there are too many perhaps but, for example, costs and timing go well together, with perhaps one other separate, numbered, section dealing with any final topics before moving on.

The principles here are similar to those for handling costs. Matters such as timing must be made completely clear and all possibilities of misunderstanding or omission avoided.

Bear the need for individuality and a tailored approach in mind; for instance, a biographical note about yourself or colleagues needs to be tailored to any specific proposal where who is actually involved in work is a factor affecting decisions to buy. Never use a "standard CV" here, incidentally; they too must be tailored to a specific client in a way that highlights those aspects of experience and so on that will be seen as desirable by that client.

Closing statement (or summary)

The final section must act to round off the document and it has a number of specific jobs to do. Its first, and perhaps most important, task is to summarise. All the threads must be drawn together and key aspects emphasised. A summary fulfils a number of purposes:

- It is a useful conclusion for all readers and should ensure the proposal ends on a note that they can easily agree is an effective summary. Because this is often the most difficult part of the document to write, it is also a part that can impress dispro-portionately. Readers know good summarising is not easy and they respect the writer who achieves it. It is a clear sign of professional competence.

- It is useful too in influencing others around the decision maker, who may study the summary but not go through the whole proposal in detail.
- It ensures the final word, and the final impression left with the reader, is about benefits and value for money.

In addition, it can be useful to:

- Recap key points (as well as key benefits).
- Stress that the proposals are, in effect, the mutual conclusions of both parties (if this is so).
- Link to action, action dates and details of contact (although this could equally be dealt with in the covering letter).
- Invoke a sense of urgency (you will normally hope for things to be tied down promptly but, ultimately, need to respect the prospect's timing).

A conventional summary appears at the end of the proposal, but an "Executive summary" is placed at the start of the document to do much the same job as one at the end. In part it is a matter of taste (or of what the client wants — ask), sometimes we can use both. The only other guide that seems useful is that a traditional summary (at the end) is best for the person involved in the proposal. They will read it through and this positioning provides the most logical explanation. For recommenders or others less involved, the executive summary may be preferred. Whichever is used it must be well written, and remember a short final word is necessary even when the main summary is placed early on.

Additional information

Two things are key here. First are *appendices*. It is important that proposals, as with any document, flow. The argument they present must proceed logically and there must be no distractions from the developing picture. Periodically, there is sometimes a need to go into deep detail. Especially if this is technical, tedious or if it involves numerous figures — however necessary the content may be — such detail should not slow and interrupt the flow of the argument. Such information can usefully be referred to at the appropriate point, but with a note that the "chapter and verse" of it appears in an appendix. Be specific, saying for example: "This detail will be found in Appendix 2: *Costs and timing*, which appears on page 21".

This arrangement can be used for a variety of elements: from terms and conditions to details inherent in the project. It can also apply to visual elements (for example, the photographs or plans an architect may use to exemplify what they say). Careful consideration is needed here not only about where to put things, but also what to use as illustrations — there needs to be a good reason, a link to what is being said and, almost always when illustrations are within the text, an explanatory caption.

Does a proposal need a covering letter?

Yes, it does. Always. In part it is a courtesy, yet the content of the letter is important, and more so for more complex situations and more elaborate proposals. It will, if it is interesting, be the first thing that is read. It sets the scene for the rest of the message and can usefully project something of the personality of the writer. So it must say more than "here is the promised proposal" (a compliments slip could do that) and is a useful place to add emphasis, perhaps instilling a sense of urgency, touching on results or setting the scene for any meeting you hope will follow.

Next, assuming proposals arrive safely and are read, there is another possibility that their use may link to that needs some thought.

The presentation of proposals

Once in front of the prospect, proposals must do their work alone, although they may be followed up in numerous ways: by letter, e-mail, telephone and so on (persistence here can pay dividends). Incidentally, consider carefully the e-mailing of proposals. This can be satisfactory, especially in sending something to people you know well (or if asked), but it does not put something as smart as a bound document on their desk. Speed may be of the essence sometimes, but you can always follow up an e-mail with a hard copy sent physically.

Once received, sometimes you know that complex proposals, especially those involving more than one person in the decision, will be the subject of formal presentations. These can happen in two main ways:

- The proposal is sent, then a presentation is made later to those who have (or should have!) read the document.

- The presentation is made first, with the detailed proposal being left as a permanent reminder of the presentation's content.

If such an arrangement is made in advance, then the proposal needs to reflect what it is. For example, you may need more detail in a proposal that has to stand on its own than one that follows a presentation. It might sometimes be possible to (with the prospect's agreement) delay completing the proposal until after a presentation; allowing the inclusion of any final elements stemming from any feedback arising during the presentation meeting. Alternatively, you can issue a revised version at this stage, either amending or adding an appendix.

Certainly there should be a close parallel between the two entities so that it is clear how anything being said at a presentation relates to the proposal. Rarely should any of the proposals be read out verbatim. What is usually most important is for additional explanation, examples and exemplification of what has been written to be given verbally.

It may cause confusion if, say, a proposal with eight main headings is discussed at a meeting with nine or ten items being run through (certainly without explanation). It is helpful if you can organise it so that the job of preparing the proposal and the presentation overlap and are kept close.

A final idea here may be useful: more than one company I know print out — for themselves — a "presentation copy" of the proposal in a larger-than-normal format or type size. This enables it to be easily referred to by someone standing in presentation style at a meeting. It also gives additional space to annotate the document with any additional notes that will help to guide the presentation along precisely. But remember that page numbers will be different on the different versions and do not let this cause confusion.

On your feet

Everything that contributes to the overall effect is important. For example, always be on time for a presentation, you cannot afford for it to start with any negative thought in the minds of those to whom you are presenting. The skills of formal presentation are beyond our brief here, but make no mistake the quality of how this is done matters. Time must be taken to prepare (the most common excuse I hear for poor presentations is that *there wasn't time to prepare*), and it must be executed well. Do not use pages from a proposal as visual aids. Many poor ones, that have far too much text on them, are originated this way — it is worth the effort to tailor-make any necessary slides.

This area may be worth separate study: I have written generally on it in *The Management Speakers' Handbook* and on a fresh use to visualising presentations in *Killer Presentations* (written with Nick Oulton, who is the ultimate guru on such matters). Both are published by How-to-Books. Both books describe presentations as "the business equivalent of an open goal". The boxed paragraph below illustrates the kind of thing *Killer Presentations* is designed to provide an antidote to:

Imagine: He who must be listened to stands at the front of the room, surrounded by equipment and with the screen glowing behind him. The audience is spellbound. The little company logo at the corner of the screen fascinates them. Every time the presenter clicks the computer mouse, and sends another yellow bullet point shuttling onto the screen from stage left, their attention soars. One slide replaces another, then another replaces that and another ... but you get the idea. Enough. All are bland, all are simple checklists, yet he who must be listened to finds them riveting; certainly he spends most of his time looking over his shoulder at the screen rather than at the audience. There is so much text on some slides that they are like pages out of a book. And an unsuitably small typeface compounds the effect and overburdens the minds of the audience. So he reads them, verbatim, more slowly than the audience does and with a tone that leads one to suspect that he is seeing them for the first time. It becomes akin to a bureaucratic rain dance: a mantra and format is slavishly, indeed unthinkingly, followed — yet at the end no one is truly satisfied. The opportunity — the open goal — is missed.

You may have been on the receiving end of such presentations; even the best proposals do not make up for them. A final thought here: I hear numbers of reports these days of clients reaching the point of scheduling a presentation and saying in effect to the supplier, *"Don't bring your marketing people"*. Presentations must reflect the nitty-gritty of working together and it is the people who will do the work that must play the key roles.

Now, two overall rules about proposals: these are obvious but are still sometimes overlooked.

- Make sure every proposal *looks good*. Use plenty of headings, bold type and other emphasis where appropriate and set it out to look professional. Do not cramp it — if it is being passed round the client organisation, then some room for annotation is useful.
- Check it carefully — and then check it again. I know one professional firm that received back a photocopy of the title page of a proposal they had sent, returned in an envelope without even a compliments slip. The name of the client's organisation was incorrectly spelt; it was ringed in red and underneath was written *No thank you!*.

Having reviewed what a proposal should be and the detail of its content, we turn to how best to get the words down on paper.

Drafting the words

It may seem easy. Call up a "Word" document and start typing. Better still, give some thought to what you want to say and then start typing. And take care what you say, and remember what Rowland Whitehead said: *If you are an enthusiast, it communicates. And nothing communicates so much as a lack of it.*

Fine you may say, so I must take care what I say; and I do. Certainly standards have changed and improved in recent years and people are more conscious of the fragility of what they do, recognising that in any communication even the wrong choice of a few words may create misunderstanding or dilute professional image. But if one form of communication lags in the way it evidences this: that is communications in writing. Somehow this is more difficult. People find themselves originating material that is at best pedestrian and at worst formulaic, banal or containing a surfeit of jargon, officespeak and gobbledegook. Why?

Most often it is lack of thought and care. Writing usually takes place with an eye on the clock. Some text may be drawn from standard material. Others are adapted one from another; as I write this I have just received a proposal from a consultant that suddenly refers to me as Margaret half way through! Oops, but I understand how easily it can happen. Or documents reflect the — bad — writing habits of a lifetime, habits that perhaps started because there was no real guidance available as to what was best. In sessions critiquing material on business writing courses, I find that the worst examples are rarely defended. No one says: *I thought long and hard about that paragraph and I believe it is the best way to say it*; more likely they admit it is unclear or gives the wrong impression and readily seek a better turn of phrase. It is not that wrong decisions are being taken, but rather thought and care is inadequate as writing takes place on "automatic pilot".

Making it right

Good writing starts with clear intentions. If you cannot say why you are writing, then it is unlikely that you will create something satisfactory. Writing must reflect clear intentions in four main areas:

- *The message*: What it is, how it can be made clear, what effect it should have on the reader, what restrictions or opportunities the form of writing reflects (has it some space restrictions, for instance if the client has specified the nature of proposal that they want)?
- *The nature of the message*: must it inform, persuade, change attitudes or motivate; or all of these and more? Whatever the intention it — or they — must be firmly in mind as you write.
- *The reader*: What are their expectations, not only for the message itself but also for the written form (will they expect it to be long or short, clear, descriptive, jargon-free etc)? If expectations reflect a meeting already held, and found useful, then they will expect your written word to continue that good impression.

What if there is more than one reader?

A proposal has to be addressed primarily towards one person. If it tries to do six different things at once it may fail in them all. It may need to make clear the line it takes in this way, that said, there is no harm in digressing (in the text, or perhaps into an appendix) and clarifying precisely who the digression is for. It might start by saying, *For those needing more detail ...* , for instance. In this way, you can succeed at talking to more than one person and still make the whole seem well constructed and useful.

- *The image put across*: What impression should what you write give of you? Maybe you need to appear experienced, helpful, well organised and such like. The complexity here is clear. There are many factors to bear in mind and all demand an active approach; in other words, it is not sufficient to be well organised, say, you have to appear so. And could it just be that your intention is to appear better organised than you actually are?

Improvement may come through developing new habits. For example, one common fault in proposal writing is that writing is introspective: every thought (or even every paragraph or sentence) in the text starting with the words *"We"*, *"I"* or *"The firm"*, when concentration should better be on the client. Resolving to twitch every time you do this and trying to express the same thought starting with the word *"You"* (or *"your"*) may help kick-start a different, and more client-focused, style.

The written word is not transient, as is a meeting. What you write may well last, can be passed around a client's organisation and can sometimes come back to haunt you long after it is written. Have a fresh look at some recent examples in your office. Ask how they would strike you if you were the recipient. Be honest. Creating something that has real impact, and will stand out from what competitors do, can be a striking, low-cost way to improve marketing communications. Any effort it takes can pay dividends.

Letters to clients

Let us consider letters for a moment, in part to lead onto more about writing that applies generally. Letters are too easily regarded as routine, and can too often turn out to be formulaic, replete with galimatias and sesquipedalians (that is gibberish and long words). Yet writing them utilises the same overall approaches as is necessary for more complex documents if you are to create good ones.

As was said earlier, the first essential is to have clear objectives; to know why, in the fullest sense, a letter is being written. Next it is to have some real structure in mind (yes, even for short letters). This need often be no more complicated than the classic beginning, middle and end. Thus we might look at a structure, here designed to encompass letters designed to be persuasive, as follows:

- *The beginning* should command attention, spark interest and lead people into the main text.
- *The middle* should hold and develop interest, talk benefits and link to the close.
- *The end* should act to actively prompt action.

One important piece of logic, which links structure and writing, may be useful to spell out. Start with the end. In a sales letter, and a covering letter designed to accompany a proposal is certainly a sales letter, it is often a "close", something ultimately designed to prompt action in the reader. It is surely logical to decide what that action is first. For example, say you decide to try to persuade someone to agree to meet with you, then you must write a letter that is specifically designed to make that happen. You cannot write a more general letter, and then ask yourself *"how shall I finish this off?"*.

Language and style

Anything you write, a letter or a proposal, should be easy to read. Try reading something to yourself (or even out loud to a colleague) and see how it sounds and how it flows. Remember punctuation allows the reader to breathe. You should punctuate correctly, using commas, colons and semi-colons appropriately for instance, but simplistically it is straightforward to recognise that if you run out of breath when reading something, then it needs *some sort* of punctuation mark adding. The most basic rules: prefer short words to long, or, as they say in the US do not use 50 cent words to make 5 cent points. Also prefer short sentences, and remember that short paragraphs work well. A common fault in business writing is over long sentences. And very short ones can be useful. See.

Similarly, short paragraphs are easy to read and digest.

A mix of these things may be best to create a suitable flow. Certain aspects (and these are not exhaustive, but just examples) need particular care:

- *First sentences*: if I had a tenner for every enquiry response letter I have seen over the years that starts along the lines of *"Thank you very much for your enquiry, details about our services are enclosed"* I could retire tomorrow. There has to be something more interesting to say — surely?
- *Last sentences*: similarly, something like *"Assuring you of our best attention at all times"* just ahead of *"Yours sincerely"*, or other cliché conclusions are excruciating and can, again, surely be bettered.
- *Clarity*: things that are expected to be complex yet are easily and fluently explained automatically impress, and it says something about the writer when this is the case. Anything left unclear will

not always be checked by the reader, and may dilute overall meaning as well as looking uncaring. For example, what exactly does a phrase like *"personal service"* mean? Done by people? If so, spell it out.

- *Much used, but inappropriate phrases*: for example, a conference organiser recently sent me, and other speakers, a note that said *".... I am also enclosing a list of speakers' contact numbers for your perusal"*. Useful information but, in my view, perusal is the wrong word. I might refer to it if necessary, but I am unlikely to "read and study it in a careful and leisurely way", which is what peruse means. It also strikes a curiously old-fashioned note and this alone should rule the word out.
- *Useful words incorrectly used*: my personal twitch is the word unique. Nothing can be very unique, quite unique or any other sort of unique — unique means it is simply unlike anything else.
- *Bland languages*: be careful to be suitably expressive. Nothing you write about is merely *"quite"*, *"rather"* or even *"very"*, good. Sales-orientated language needs to have the courage of its convictions, if something is excellent, practical or unique say so, and then explain, descriptively, why is this so.

Again care and attention to detail is necessary. Just one word or phrase rather than another may make a difference. If you are seeking to create impact, be descriptive or differentiate — and regularly you will — find words that do just that. You are not trying to follow a long established style or reiterate old-fashioned convention, you are trying to communicate and to make what you say interesting.

Experiment. Sometimes you may find you look at what you have written and suck your teeth — *I'd better not say it like that* — because it seems too informal or is not real "business language". Maybe sometimes you should not go back, edit and produce something safer, yet more bland. Trust your powers of description. Say it and you may well find clients like it.

To quote a personal example, publisher Management Pocketbooks, having expressed interest in my idea for a book, then put the project on hold interminably (you probably know the feeling). Every follow up I made failed to get through. Finally, I wrote and sent the following, positioning it centrally alone on a sheet of letterhead:

Struggling author, patient, reliable, non-smoker seeks commissions on business topics. Novel formats preferred, but anything considered. Ideally 100 or so pages on the topic of *sales excellence* sounds good; maybe with some illustrations. Delivery of the right quantity of material — on time — guaranteed. Contact me at the above address/telephone number or let's arrange to meet on neutral ground carrying a copy of *Publishing News* and wearing a carnation.

I remember that I nearly did not send this and wondered if it was entirely suitable (I had written something else for them, but had only met the editor once). I was pleased I did as confirmation arrived in an e-mail on the following day. So some creativity can pay dividends. (You can see the result of this in *The Sales Excellence Pocketbook*.)

Make sure every piece of text, whether in a proposal or elsewhere, really works for you. If you know you offer special service, unusual value for money, and better technical expertise or communications along the way, then do not rely on people reading between the lines to get the full message, spell it out to them loud and clear. Give them something they will want to read. It is worth the time it takes. As Gene Fowler said, *Writing is easy, all you do is sit staring at blank sheet of paper until the drops of blood form on your forehead*. Yes, it does need some effort.

You must persuade yourself that writing is not a chore, but an opportunity to impress.

One more thing: proposals (and many letters, e-mails etc) must be *persuasive*. Many of the principles set out earlier about face-to-face communication can be used here and will not be repeated. By way of summary on the matter this chapter concludes with a reminder of some of the key points.

Writing to persuade

Simply saying what you want is not enough. If I sent you details of something, this book say, and said only read this, I want you to, then you might well reject the thought out of hand — shan't. But if I say that reading it might just help get your next proposal accepted rather than rejected or ignored, then you are more likely to take an interest. This illustrates the first principle. Persuasive writing must offer the reader reasons for them to agree or act that reflect their point of view, not say only why you think they should do something. Such writing demands empathy and must exhibit a style unlike any other. So, some dos and don'ts, which add to and pick up again some of the points already made:

- *Avoid* the introspective tone mentioned earlier. If every sentence, paragraph or thought begins with the word "I" — *I will ... I can ...* and worst of all *I want* — it creates a "catalogue" approach, a list of things from your own point of view, which becomes tedious and is unlikely to prompt interest in the reader. Try rewriting any such sentiment starting it with the word "You". It will sound very different. Thus: *I would like to give you ...* becomes something that begins, *Your organisation will find ...* . If the latter continues by explaining *why* what is suggested will be found interesting and how it can be valuable, better still.

- *Avoid* circumspection. A persuasive document is no place for *I think, I hope, probably, maybe* or *perhaps*. You need to have the courage of your convictions. Ideas and suggestions, or any matter on which you seek agreement, must reflect your confidence in it. So phrases such as *this will give you ...* are better. Similarly, avoid bland description. Your idea is never just *very good*. A suggested project stage should never be stated as being *quite valuable*. Use words that add drama and certitude.

- *Stress* the benefits. Remember, from earlier, how this reflects some of the jargon of the sales world. Features are factual things — tangible or intangible — about something. This section is around 700 words long, occupies one/two page(s) and deals with persuasive writing: all these points are features. Whereas benefits are things that something does for or means to people. So the benefits of reading these pages are things like: giving you an introduction to the principles of persuasive writing, helping you avoid key mistakes that will dilute the persuasive effectiveness of your writing or increasing the chances of your next proposal being accepted. Benefits should predominate. There should be sufficient benefits to persuade, they should be well expressed and, if necessary, backed up by proof or evidence.

- *Make it* readable. His has been said, but making something persuasive must not obscure the other virtues it must exhibit. As with anything else, you will need a clear beginning, middle and end. In context here the important thing is to allow your writing to project something of yourself. Make sure it is not formulaic as if out of a textbook. Whether you want to sound friendly, efficient or professional — whatever — make sure such characteristics show.

As with most writing, if you need to write something that must be persuasive it needs some preparation. Think about what you want to say. Ask yourself why anyone should agree to your idea or proposal. List the reasons; all of them. Then organise them. What are the most important things? How does one link to another? Arrange a logical argument, say something at the beginning to command attention and get the reader reading, and write to maintain interest throughout. The progression of this approach is a powerful aid to writing right and writing fast. You may ask: *Doesn't elaborate preparation just make the whole thing take longer; after all, I know my own area, is it really necessary?*.

The answer must be a firm, *yes, it is necessary*. But, in my experience, good preparation helps you write faster and means that less editing will be necessary before you complete the writing; in fact, it acts to shorten the overall job. So list the things you want to say and the points you need to make, put them in a logical order, fine-tune a bit with the overall length in mind and then write to the plan you have made. This separates the job of deciding what to write from that of *how* to express it.

A powerful start that then tails away will persuade no one. Lead with the benefits. Let features follow to explain. These pages will allow readers to *experiment with a more persuasive style* (benefit), because *it is written reflecting proven, practical approaches* (feature).

Again, further details go beyond the brief here, but, for more about this, the use of language and other aspects of preparing a proposal you could read my book *Powerful Reports and Proposals* (Kogan Page).

Next time you set out to make a case in writing perhaps you might consider some checking ... . No! Sorry. Start again: next time you send off a proposal make checking that it is not just well described, but *persuasively* described, a priority. Let me leave the final word on this topic to another writer:

> The ability to write well is the most neglected skill in business life. We all intuitively know that we need to use words well to succeed in our work, yet we continue to regard writers as specialists on the fringes of life. My contention is that writers are thinkers. Good writers are good thinkers. What business does not need good thinking at its heart? If you improve the writing ability of your company, or at least its sensitivity to language, you will improve your company's performance.

John Simmons, in the book *We, me, them and it* (Texere).

In a field such as property, this link between thinking and making a persuasive case is a sensible thing upon which to dwell.

Part 4

Maximising Results

"The best we ever heard of was the one who sold two milking machines to the farmer who only had one cow. Then this salesman helped finance the deal by taking the cow as a down payment on the two milking machines."

Herbert Prochnow

Reinforcing Your Case

12

The techniques that can help build your case, strengthen it and make it more likely to prove one that will be agreed, are, as we have already seen, many and various. There are factors that can have potentially powerful effects on what you do that do not fall exclusively under headings dealt with earlier on. Here we review some of these additional factors.

Use your colleagues to strengthen sales effectiveness

Not even the most professional person can do everything. The complexities of the property world, and of many clients, mean that some situations inevitably need the skills, expertise and experience only available through a combination of people working together. This is a fact of business life. It should not be regarded as a sign of weakness and avoided but used where appropriate to secure sales that might be unachievable any other way.

So who do you work with? There are a number of options: a colleague, someone with different experience or skills, a member of technical support or service, staff from research or a member of the management team. The key to making two-handed meetings work is planning and, if necessary, rehearsing. You must think about and agree who will do what and who, above all, will be in the chair, directing the meeting and bringing the other in as appropriate. Whose meeting it is must be clear, and clear in advance.

Never go out to a client in a team without sitting down and talking through how you will handle the meeting. Decide who will introduce who and how. You need to be clear how you will explain to the client the need for two of you, or more, to be there. If one of you knows the buyer, they should introduce the newcomer, always making it clear that their experience or expertise makes their contribution valuable *to the client*. Never give the impression that things are being handed over to someone less important or less qualified to assist than the prime contact. A suggested agenda for such a meeting may be very useful to help keep it organised. Do not give the impression of crowding or pressurising the client by arriving "mob-handed", the reason needs to be stated in client terms: *So that we can go through some of the technical detail for you and take things further without delay I have brought along my colleague ... who will ... .*

If you have worked out in advance how you will handle things, such a meeting can be as effective as any other and, in fact, may be more so, or at least allow good additional factors to be brought into play. Good teamwork is always impressive. The client will draw conclusions about how your organisation works and your likely service and quality from his observation of how you go about things — hence the importance of preparation and rehearsal. The meeting must be "seamless", that is handover from one person to another on your side must be smooth and without hesitation. You cannot afford to say things like: *I think that's all on that, now John you were going to deal with such and such matters weren't you?* What you do between you must appear fluid and certain and must end by giving the client all they want as certainly as any other meeting.

The technique of building up the credentials of someone working with you to boost their image with a client, even if they are less senior or experienced that the person introducing them is called "delegating up". A concept worth noting, it works well.

Consider also small advantages of working together. One may be the designated note taker, freeing the other to concentrate on the conversation. One may be able to think through some problem while a colleague is talking and so resolve a point quickly and impressively on the spot. While you should not now suddenly resolve never to go to a meeting on your own again, do consider those few key meetings that can benefit from this approach and use them carefully — they can sometimes produce disproportionately good results.

Develop a fluency with figures

I once saw a buyer running rings round a salesman with whom he was negotiating. The buyer kept tapping away at a large desktop calculator and then quoting figures to find fault with the salesman's argument. It sounded very authoritative and the salesman took the figures as gospel and, because his cost-effectiveness argument seemed flawed, agreed to a larger discount than he had originally intended. Yet the buyer did not have the calculator plugged in, the figures he was quoting were pure bluff; but he still achieved his objective.

Few professionals will admit to being weak at finance, but some of us are simply not sufficiently numerate to cope sufficiently quickly and certainly — with the sort of situation depicted above. If you are in this category and feel any kind of vulnerability in this way, albeit only a small one, then you need to compensate.

How do you do this? More training may be necessary, but here let me make a simpler point. If there are any areas where your ability to project and deal with your case is weaker than you would like, then you must prepare what you do in those areas more thoroughly. Make a whole range of calculations before the meeting. Work out every kind of permutation you think may need dealing with. Turn things into more a manageable form — using graphs is a useful way of making figures easier to follow. Use modern technology: maybe a programmable calculator can help, or maybe you need a laptop computer with you. Make sure you are not lagging in this important area.

The property business, and therefore the selling that takes place within it, are about money. Accountants may deal with such issues seemingly without the need for thought (although someone once said that there are three kinds of accountant; those who can add up and those that cannot!). You do not need to be a qualified accountant to be successful at selling, but you do need a degree of numeracy that matches the needs of the work you do and, in many situations, nothing less will do.

Be good on your feet

This was touched on in the chapter about writing proposals, but is worth a word more. It is a universal trend that more and more situations are demanding that those that do the selling are not only good at presenting their case one to one, across the desk, but also on their feet in formal, stand-up presentations. The buyer may increasingly be the Board, the staff of a department, a committee or a group of some other sort. In some areas, people talk of the "beauty parade", and business does not come without passing over this necessary hurdle.

Presentation skills are not everyone's stock in trade and there is a great deal of difference between presenting sitting comfortably across the table from someone you know well and facing an apparently hostile or indifferent group of, say, a dozen people whose expectations may be unclear. Hence the saying: *The human brain is a wonderful thing — it starts working on the day you are born — goes on and on — and only stops on the day you have to speak in public.* If you are not good at presenting, but have to do it, or may have to in the future, then it is a skill you simply must acquire. Not everyone will ever be a great orator, but nearly everyone can learn to make a workmanlike presentation, and anyone's style will improve with some thought.

The first rule is preparation. So is the second and the third. Think about what you want to say, think about what order you will say it in, think about how you will say it — from tone of voice to visual aid to dramatic pause. And arrange it with the classic beginning, middle and end. Make notes, not to read from (this is for most people rather difficult to do fluently), but to guide you. Practice, practice, practice. Once you are sure you are clear what you are going to do and how, it will be easier.

Make no mistake, a good presenter has an edge on the poor. People do not say, *What a pity they are a poor presenter, never mind I am sure their ideas are good*. They are more likely to say, *That seems poor*; full stop. So it is an important skill and worth some separate study, as there are a good many "tricks of the trade" to get your mind round. It is too big a topic to do justice to here (but may repay investigation and study). Add good presentation skills to your armoury and it will stand you in good stead generally for the future as well as in selling terms.

Use your authority

Clients need to see you (or certainly to see someone!) as their prime contact with authority to deal with all aspects of their business with your organisation. This does not mean that you must be the only person from the company they ever meet. But it does mean you have to be careful to introduce others in a positive context. It is one thing to introduce someone to augment what you do, by providing a necessary higher level of technical information or expertise, for instance; it is quite another to seek help, advice or decision in a manner that indicates a clear and inappropriate gap in your authority.

So it is helpful to ensure that you are able to deal with as much as possible that can occur with clients, to position yourself as the key contact and let them see you as the one who makes the decisions regarding their business. Any necessary checks can be made in the background, preferably before the meeting. Be seen to be in charge and your authority will be challenged less. Where sales overlaps into actually doing work for a client, your position and the arrangement of the whole team involved must be clear; and organised to create a suitable profile for all.

Consider swapping clients with your colleagues

No one person is ideally suited to sell, equally successfully, to everyone in the world. Sometimes clients will not respond because they will only do business if whoever is representing the company exhibits special skills or characteristics. Or it may be that special technical knowledge is necessary. Alternatively, it may be that only a good match in terms of factors such as age, sex or experience are acceptable. It could also be that some buyers just do not like you (I know, it is almost unbelievable — what a thought — surely everyone likes you?) For most people, if they are honest, this is simply not true, none of us get on equally well with everyone and sometimes it is purely a matter of style or personality.

Any factor may be incompatible; I once worked with a company where one client said he would like to do business but would only do so if whoever came to talk to them was: *longer in the tooth and shorter in the hair* than his first contact. He liked the organisation and what was being offered but, in a very traditional business with primarily older people at the senior levels, preferred to deal with someone older, less fashionable and more experienced. At least he said so, and, with some judicious staffing, business was obtained as a result. So be it, the client is always right. Someone has to worry about allocating the right client to the right member of the team.

If, however, you find this has not happened and you have apparently intractable problems with a particular prospect, then perhaps you should consider swapping that prospect with one handled by one of your colleagues. This can sometimes break the deadlock. A new face may be seen in a different light. The client who would not buy from you may then buy and you may move on and get business from someone new. Refusing to recognise the problem will simply compound the difficulty, whereas some informal networking around the organisation can pay dividends.

Follow-up and Persistence 13

Certainly, as we have already seen, you are unlikely to maximise success in selling without some measure of organisational skills. There is more to winning business than simply handling meetings in the right way. Often the process is multi-stage, many things need following up, progressing from stage to stage until the client has satisfactorily gone through the stages and processes they feel are necessary to making a decision. Successful people recognise this fact and become adept at dealing with the follow-up action required. Here we investigate these skills.

Handling a multi-stage contact

Not every sale or piece of business is secured by one meeting, however well handled. In many situations, the process is multi-staged and this may take many forms. For example, a enquiry received through a telephone call may lead to an appointment; at the meeting the prospect may indicate that another meeting, perhaps one in which you need to involve a colleague, will be necessary in order to progress matters; at the second meeting the prospect agrees that what they are seeing looks good and is agreeable to the submission of a quotation (or sometimes a written proposal); with the proposal submitted it may be necessary to arrange another meeting to tie things down, and this could take the form of a formal presentation to the Board or to a buying committee; after that maybe another meeting and ... there could well be more. This sounds daunting, and indeed it can be, and the lead time involved can vary too, making for additional complications.

From initial meeting to order may take days, weeks, months or many months, and a longer time may be no reflection on the way things have been conducted in the interim, it may be perfectly logical from the point of view of the client. As I write this, I am reminded of some work I booked recently that took almost two years to see through to that point; somewhat unusual in consultancy, but, as with any order, welcome on the day confirmation finally came through.

However many stages there may be *en route* to an order and whatever they may be, it is key that you progress the contact and steer it firmly from one stage to the next. Perhaps the longer the lead time, the greater is the need to do this systematically. The effect on the client is sequential and cumulative. Unless each stage is effective and they are persuaded to take things further, the process may falter and no order will result.

As time and effort must be put in to get from stage to stage, the further along the sequence things come to a halt, the greater the opportunity cost (waste!). Think back, for instance, to chapter 11 about written proposals: the time these take to prepare and write is considerable, and an architect may have additional time and cost tied up in preparing draft plans and suggestions. On the other hand, the amount of time that is spent on follow-up activity, making sure that you move firmly from one stage to the next, maintaining contact in the gaps, need not be great, even though the elapsed time may be many months. During my two-year lead time mentioned above, just two brief meetings and about 10 telephone calls, e-mails or letters were involved while I tried to retain some patience and remain optimistic.

Without a doubt there is some business that goes to those people who are more systematic and persistent than their competitors. Being persistent is well worthwhile, but it is not altogether easy. Psychologically the contacts that fill the gaps can be awkward to make. What do you say when the prospect's secretary has told you three times in a week that, *They're so busy*? Well, you take it face value, at least to start with, and try to find out the best time to make contact. And you phone again. You cannot afford to be paranoid, you need a thick skin and if you operate this way, making a firm date in your diary system so that you keep up the contact, then you will win more and lose touch with less.

Use one contact to arrange the next

The closing objective at the end of every contact where ongoing contact is necessary is to arrange the next contact. You can either ask: *Can we get together again once you have those figures — when will that be?*, or you can suggest: *Can I suggest we meet again once you have those figures — what about one day early next week?"* Whatever the route, the objective is to have specific agreement to a dated and timed further meeting (or whatever the next contact needs to be) before you walk out of the door or put down the telephone. You will not always succeed, but sometimes it will secure a commitment and that removes the need to follow up later, something which may be more awkward. If things are progressing well, if the client has expressed an interest, agreed that you should submit a proposal, why not move on one more step and agree the date of another meeting — all while they are in the mood to say yes?

Make good use of the telephone

A note of caution is due here. It is easy to pick up the phone and make a call; easier than ever now when no meeting (or, I notice, training course!) seems complete without the occasional ringing of the now ubiquitous mobile telephone. But too often the dialling finger is put in gear before the brain; always ask yourself why you are phoning and make sure you have a reason — an objective you can state in client terms. That said, it is a convenient and useful way of keeping in touch.

The telephone is so much taken for granted that its correct use may have been forgotten. The following may seem basic, but it is important and getting matters absolutely right can increase a call's effectiveness. If you want to come over to the listener clearly then remember that the telephone exaggerates the rate of speech and heightens the tone. You must talk into the mouthpiece in a clear normal voice (if you are a woman it may help to pitch your voice lower than normal). It is surprising how many things can interfere with the simple process of talking directly into the mouthpiece: smoking, trying to write, or holding a file open for instance. There are other hazards to be avoided: a noisy office or a bad line. So remember:

- Speak a little slower than in normal conversation.
- It is said that if you smile it affects how you sound positively.
- Use a warm tone of voice.
- Put the emphasis on the key points.
- Be positive.
- Be concise, clients' time is valuable.

- Avoid jargon.
- Use gestures as you would face-to-face, as it will change how you sound.
- Think about and project a clear, natural tone.

Above all, remember the client *cannot see you*, obvious perhaps but it does mean your voice must do all the work. If you bear all these in mind, the telephone will cease to be routine and will become a valuable element in the process of keeping in touch.

This kind of detail may appear pedantic, but the perceived profile of a professional is important: and telephone contacts can too often have a "dashed off" element to them. As with many people, I receive several messages on voicemail each week in which either the name or number of the caller is rattled out so fast as to be completely lost; it is all too easy to say to yourself, *do these people care at all?* If such occurs when professional advice or expertise is being sold it is all the more damaging.

Drop them a line

Some people think of themselves as predominantly face-to-face people. They are more comfortable talking to clients than with other forms of communication and have a distaste for what they see as the chore of putting things in writing. Telephoning is the middle course, and undeniably provides a useful method of keeping in touch. But it is transient, in other words, while it is a useful reminder of you and your products and company, it may well be quickly forgotten. A written message on the other hand is permanent, or at least potentially long lasting. Therefore, it can potentially have a greater effect. Besides, it pays to ring the changes.

There are a number of ways and occasions when a letter is useful:

- To announce an intention to telephone (and perhaps to include the reason why).
- To announce a new development, proofs of a new advertisement, an organisational change, a new appointment (a short note and a copy of something such as a press release or newsletter giving the details may be appropriate here).
- To send an item of interest to them (a press cutting, perhaps, or some item of market intelligence that is beneficial to them).

- To invite them to an event (a press function, an exhibition, a social function).
- You can even get some value in terms of a reminder from more mundane matters such as chasing an unpaid invoice, which has to be done awkward though it may be: remember that it is not a sale until the money is in the bank (and the cheque has cleared!).

You must judge the frequency of contact carefully, something dropping through the post every five minutes like so much confetti will seem wasteful and may be regarded as exerting undue pressure. An occasional written reminder, especially if it is in a form that is useful to the client, works well. Not all written messages are now sent in hard copy form, hence the next heading.

Sending an e-mail

Whatever did we do before we had e-mail? Few, if any, technical innovations have swept the business world so quickly and so completely and the speed and ease of contact they allow is invaluable. The very nature of e-mail is different from other written communication, it has inherited the sense of urgency that was once the preserve of the fax.

E-mail also seems to have developed a certain informality, sometimes so much so that it loses clarity (how often do you have to reply to an e-mail just to check what it was really saying?). People write what are perhaps best described as external memos, with less of the formal headings and layout that characterises business correspondence and this is done not only between people where some relationship has been built up; think carefully before you omit or reduce the formalities, but there will be situations where you conclude rightly that it is not necessary. As e-mail can be deleted at the touch of a button, it should not be the only form of maintaining contact, nor should it be regarded as creating a permanent reminder.

Creating and Managing Client Relationships

Now we move beyond simple persistent contact to ensure things are not lost by default and neglect. People do business, not organisations (although they may be the legal entity involved). Relations between the people who interface at the sales stage of a business relationship are very important. It is especially important when you hope the business will be ongoing, and that regular business will continue to come from a particular client; this is presumably the hope of everyone in the property sector (even estate agents recognise that people move more than once). Another thing to encourage here is referrals.

One point should be made clear here. Traditionally many people in property, certainly the more consultative, have regarded there as being to strands of communications with clients. First, communication must be persuasive — it is selling (even if euphemisms such as business development are used). Then, if business is secured, it is seen as changing: with communications being with a client, rather than a prospect, and being one involved with doing the work, whatever that is. These days, a better view is one that sees the communications track splitting in two at the point of agreement (think of an upside down tuning fork). Here selling does not stop and change to something else; rather two parallel threads continue alongside one another: one is selling, continuing as opportunities are sought for future work, and the other is what is necessary to manage the client relationship and the work being done.

This is not something that you cannot rely on just happening, the next few headings review how you can make the likelihood more certain.

Create a role for yourself in your clients' businesses

Clients will do business with you on a regular basis if they value your offering, approve your back-up service and more so if they respect and get on with you personally. But you can create a more powerful bond than this; you do not just want to be an occasional contact, however pleasant they find you. You want to position yourself appropriately with regard to their business. Some of this positioning may involve peripheral elements to the real nature of your business. However, if you can become regarded as, say, a valuable source of competitive intelligence as well as a professional operator, this will create a larger role for you.

Such a role can be stronger still. For example, many property people have an advisory role inherent within their job, and this can go further than just a little competitive intelligence. One sales person I have dealt with regularly for some years has cultivated this kind of role very usefully. He sells print. I buy my business stationery, business cards and invoices from him. He also produces brochures I need for direct mail promotion of seminars and, where my client work involves print he may also be involved. His advice is excellent, whether it involves the additional cost of illustrations, how to choose sizes to avoid waste of paper in cutting, or explaining the differences between six different ways of varnishing a brochure to create exactly the right finish, he is helpful and his advice is sound. He will spend as much time over something on a speculative project for a client of mine, where he knows they will get a quote from a printer they already use and the chances of his receiving the work are less, as he does on more certain jobs. Because he gives freely of his time in this way and because his advice is good, I would be reluctant to do any project involving print without having a word with him. More than this, I feel some obligation to involve him on new work because of time he has spent in the past. The relationship makes sense both ways. This kind of process can be evolved for all aspects of the property business, although in an advice business not too much must be given away upfront or the relationship will change and profitability will take a dive.

More to the point, it becomes difficult for competition to break in on such a relationship. If you are more than a "just a supplier", if you have a role in your client's business, then the bond will be strong. It takes a while to work your way into such a position, but doing so is time well spent. And it helps to think consciously about the kind of role you are seeking to fulfil — which may involve a simple thread of activity as the example above shows — and then work towards it. As with so much else in the process of generating new business successfully, such a relationship does not just happen.

Control the "chat"

Selling can sometimes be more successful if you have a good relationship with the client and, while you do not have to like them all, some may well become, or become close to, being real friends. Friendship may make some aspects of the sales process more difficult, as with closing, for instance. What is most important is that, like each other or not, there should be a professional respect between the two parties.

There is a story told of a salesman being asked to explain how he has managed to retain a client for so long, regularly receiving good business from him. He says it is all on account of the good relationship they have, that the client is madly keen on golf and that as long as he checks how this is going, lets him recount how he won the weekend tournament, the relationship stays good and business continues. When this same client is asked why he does business with the salesman, he speaks highly of his professionalism, his technical expertise, his product knowledge and good service — but ends up by saying: *I just wish he would not go on so long about the golf!*

There is a serious point here. It is quite difficult to draw the line between taking an interest and getting on and being a bore and wasting client's precious time. Where a professional relationship is involved, one that may necessitate considerable resources and time being spent with or on behalf of clients (as with an architect or surveyor, say), it is worth drawing this line carefully. Be careful not to let a client's enthusiasm for a shared interest or any other distraction become too time-consuming. When they wake up to it, their loyalty may evaporate very fast.

The moral is clear; be careful to balance the chatty elements of the conversation with the business elements. Too little informality and the relationship can be stifled to the detriment of doing business, too much chat and you will be seen as a time waster — in which case it will waste your time too and reduce your productivity.

Deliver!

This one word heading is not meant in the sense of getting a physical product delivered safely and on time (although if that applies, it must be done). Rather it implies the personal delivery of elements of what the client gets that are very much bound up in the person they deal with. By way of example, the following are key and make the point:

- *Keep promises*: Always do what you say you will and do it by when you say you will. If you promise to get back to them by three o'clock with some figures, then you must do exactly that. And preferably do it before three. If you should find that something promised will, in the event, not be possible, then you must make contact *before* the deadline and rearrange — with an apology — an alternative arrangement. Better still, always consider carefully the deadlines you set, it is better to give yourself a little more time and then better it, than to be late. This may be especially true if the action you plan is dependent on others, in which case some contingency for their possible imperfections may be wise.

- *Make your administration perfect*: Always ensure that documentation connected with your personal contact with the client is right. This may be something simple you originate, such as a message to confirm an appointment. Or it may be more complex and originate elsewhere in your company. Make no mistake: if anything, up to and including the invoice, is incorrect, you are the one likely to be blamed. From the client's point of view this is only logical, and it is no help to lay blame on others if the client sees you as fronting the team. So details must be correct, everything must be in its place and, above all, it must all be clear and understandable.

Maintain a reputation of reliability with your clients and this can reinforce your position with them, especially for a service organisation. It also acts to reduce uncertainty, which is important in many businesses, an estate agent being one example. Make them think not just twice but three or four times before they risk dealing with a competitor — who you make them fear may turn out not to deliver as you do. It is important before, during and after the sale process. Brochures and quotations must be presented correctly, information prepared for and left with the client at the end of a meeting, and follow-up documentation and action of all sorts — all must deliver in exactly the way the client wants.

Finally, it is worth remembering the old maxim that if you deliver a little more than promised, people notice, appreciate and remember.

Sort queries/complaints effectively

The concept of "delivering" — with a capital D — explored above applies equally to dealing with difficulties. Before going any further it is worth stressing that there should not be many queries and complaints; things should be handled correctly in the first place. Indeed, take time to get things right in the first place and you will not need to take time to resolve any problem.

But let us be realistic: even in the best-run companies there may be a few negative things to sort out and when it does happen you can score points by responding fast, sorting it out and achieving the desired results quickly and certainly. This is true of simple queries. A figure is inappropriately omitted from a proposal and needs to be added. Done quickly, with an apology rather than an excuse, and with good grace, then very little problem may be caused.

If something more serious has arisen and a complaint is made, this must be picked up and handled well. A well-chosen approach followed through logically is useful here, as the natural human reactions (such as saying it is not your fault, or starting to argue) can easily make things worse.

Though it is, hopefully, not something that occurs too often it is worth spelling out the principles involved. The following techniques should deal with the majority of complaints and action, whether on the telephone or face-to-face:

1. *Listen* to all the facts, reassure the complainant frequently with, *Yes, I understand*, and let them run out of steam. This gives you time to think about what you will say, and what action to take. Write down the details and make sure you get the person's name, telephone number and contact details clear, early on, as it may well not be someone you already know.
2. *Sympathise* and make someone feel that you would feel the same way if you were in their shoes. Show them there will be no argument. Never interrupt with, *But*. Apologise, at least for their state of mind, and yet do so without necessarily taking the blame (where this lies may not be established yet).
3. *Clarify* and make sure you have *all the facts right*. Still keep away

from arguing — the truth about the complaint may not be as it seems at first. Avoid doubt phrases such as: *you claim or as I understand it*, which make the client feel they are being disbelieved; that will only make them reinforce their complaint.

4. *Summarise* the complaint, which will serve to check that you have all the facts, and reassure the client that you understand their problem — it will get them "nodding" with you for the first time.

    If at this point you have to check or investigate, it may be necessary to call back; certainly you should avoid keeping people holding on for long. You need to explain exactly what will now happen and how long it will take (a promise you must then keep — *I will be back to you within an hour*). If you do not know them, it will help the situation if you use your name and, if possible, assure the person you will call them back personally. Anything less may sound evasive.

5. *Answering a justified complaint.* If possible, accept the blame and apologise unreservedly. Remember that the client sees you as personifying the whole company. State what action you will take to put things right, even if your own action is merely to pass the complaint on (never downwards, however).

It is useful to give some perceived concession if possible, but not too much. You should try to do more than the minimum needed to put things right. Thank the client for bringing this to your attention, and follow it up.

6. *Answering an unjustified complaint.* If the client is mistaken or has got the wrong end of the stick, be diplomatic. If it is a misunderstanding, you can blame yourself for not being clearer, and the documentation, a letter, the invoice, whatever, for being confusing. Try to allow the other person to correct themselves and "save face", for example: *Do you have the e-mail confirming the dates in front of you?* They may see the error before you have to point it out.

7. *Complaint follow-up.* You must always do whatever you promised to do for the client and must advise whoever else needs to know about the complaint (in some organisations via a formal complaint form). But there is something else to remember.

A complaint is still a contact with a client, often a close one, and one initiated by the client. It can often be developed from a complaining call into something that promotes good feelings about the organisation, which can enhance the business relationship. The easiest way to achieve this is to follow the technique above, and then do something extra. Make a follow-up note in the diary to ensure that you (personally) check that matters have been resolved and that whatever the next communication may be, that this is not reduced in effectiveness by the past experience.

Be appreciative

While you should never expect a client's automatic support, you should show appreciation of business received. Clients do not "support" you, they do business with you only because you deliver in some way, meet a need and do so in a way that offers better value for money than any competitor. Your professionalism, good service and expertise may, of course, be a part of the basis on which they make their decision. So too may their respect or liking for you, but to talk of support is the wrong way of putting it; certainly you should not say to a client, *Thank you for your support*, as this characterises the business relationship in wholly the wrong way.

Nor should you state thanks in a way that appears to grovel. Too much gushing thanks can be read as desperation for business and you do not want clients to see you in that light. Thanks must be clear, sincere and business-like. Thanks can be said, but may mean more if it is put in writing. It is pleasant to receive a letter that has been written for no other reason than to express thanks; apart from the fact of the thanks, it shows respect for the clients and that you feel the business relationship is worth some trouble to maintain. And sometimes it needs to be more tangible — a drink or a meal may be appropriate. This can be positioned as a chance to relax together after the work and the decision that has been made, and is often better done in a way that rewards past client loyalty and is not in danger of being seen as a bribe given with the hope of winning future orders.

A continuing relationship can promote a continuing flow of orders — repeat business. But more of the same may not be achieving everything you can in terms of either revenue or profitability; increasing the levels of repeat business necessitates other approaches, for instance to sell the product or service range. Such are the topics of the next set of headings.

Achieving client profitability

The concept of sales productivity has already been mentioned, the more you achieve in terms of revenue from clients the more productive — and profitable — you will be; it is always easier and may be less time-consuming to sell more to people you already know than to find still more prospects. More sales, and particularly more sales across the range of products or services you sell will also increase profitability, although discounting price or fees for larger or regular clients may reduce margins somewhat. Some analysis of clients, certainly of the larger or those who are potentially larger, is useful to see whether there are further possibilities to sell more over the above by simply keeping in touch and maintaining contact.

There are two key factors to consider in such an analysis, which can be easily done; they are the product range and the different buying points in a particular client. You will be familiar with the first, your product range may be simple — products A, B and C — or there may be greater complexity and you may do better to consider groups of products (in the way a surveyor might divide their services into those for commercial and domestic clients, and then a more detailed breakdown).

By different buying points I mean people — buyers — and also places. A corporate client may be organised in two divisions, both with a buyer for your products, or have offices in several locations, or you may have opportunities to do business separately with two or more departments — which focus on existing and future properties perhaps.

It is comparatively simple to plot these two factors together on a matrix chart (see figure 14.1) which allows you to fill in either levels of business you are already doing, would like to do (potential) or look at their total sourcing for some product line or area of work. Such an analysis quickly shows where there are any gaps in your coverage, helping review whether you are seeing all the right people, and looking at what you are achieving with each. It flags additional opportunities that might otherwise be overlooked.

This is especially helpful with large clients. A healthy level of business can disguise opportunities: you may look at the overall, large, revenue figure and simply say, good — missing the fact that there are additional possibilities. Where the client knows you, likes what you do and contact is continuing, this technique can help focus future time and effort with the client and result in action plans that increase sales results.

		BUYING POINT A	BUYING POINT B	BUYING POINT C	TOTAL
P R O D U C T S	1				
	2				
	3				
	4				
TOTAL					

Figure14.1 Matrix chart

The next headings also investigate the idea of selling more to those people you already know.

The "gin and tonic" technique

This description refers to the linking of one purchase with another and represents a simple and effective way of increasing sales. The name comes from the sale of drinks. If someone walks into a shop and asks for a bottle of gin, whisky, vodka or whatever, the sales-orientated assistant should automatically ask: *How many mixers would you like?* and will very often sell a dozen bottles of tonic water in addition to the original item requested if they do so.

This idea has wide application. You have to work it out and experiment with the links that can be used in this way around your product range. The following examples will suggest the possibilities:

* Property purchase and mortgage finance.
* Building plans and assistance to obtain planning permission.
* A basic survey and further detailed investigation.

Such a list can doubtless be considerably expanded, and made specific to your business. The additional purchase may be immediate, two items being bought together, or a second purchase may follow later (in which case a note to link the two things must be kept). However it can be made to occur, it can be made to increase revenue. All it often takes is a simple question. So watch out for all the possible links and use them. Make it a reflex and you can increase sales and do so with comparative ease.

Build on success

Most of your clients will be happy with you most of the time and, although a few may have the occasional complaint, let us assume this is the case. There will also be some moments when client relationships are at an extra high point. Something has happened to make the client think particularly well of you, your company or your offering. This may include such things as:

- Exceptional service (by you), including the efficient righting of an error.
- Particular satisfaction, for example your advice, product or service has solved or helped solve some problems, or let them take advantage of a timely opportunity.
- Experience of back-up service, resulting in a saving of time or money perhaps.
- Something unexpected, a query they assumed would be troublesome, dealt with painlessly or a technical possibility they had not realised was available.

Many things may occur with clients you deal with regularly, and it is always worth your advancing follow-up action or moving on to develop new initiatives at such a moment.

For example, a project completed satisfactorily may indicate the moment to move on to selling more of the range. Clients are more likely to commit when they are pleased not just with you, but with themselves. At a time when business is good, your contact at an account has just been promoted or some initiative they have taken has worked out well, they could be a little more receptive to what you have been trying, perhaps with limited previous success, to interest them in.

Be a source of ideas

It is often not sufficient to be a professional and operate efficiently. Clients expect more and certainly they like to get more. Positioning yourself as an advisor has already been mentioned, for some clients the way to really win their loyalty is to be seen as a source of ideas. It has been said of management that they are not paid to have all the good ideas necessary to run their part of the business well, but they are surely paid to make sure there are sufficient new ideas to keep up or keep ahead. Similarly with people handling sales and clients, you do need to be on the look out for any ideas that might help your client's business — especially those that link to your work with them.

For example, this is a field in which the initial ideas of a client wanting an architect to design a building can often act as a spur to discussions that take things further — the house extension going from one to two stories is a simple example.

Such things need an active, creative approach and often necessitate being a little more involved in the client's business. Some professionals are very successful at this and get themselves into a position where clients telephone them — *What do you think about so and so?* — consulting them at an early stage on areas of mutual interest. Such an approach thus has two benefits: first, directly creating new sales opportunities. And second, creating an atmosphere in which clients are more likely to come to you, to ask to involve you at an early stage, all of which may extend sales possibilities beyond the basic requirements.

Helpful Attitudes

We now move towards the end of this review with the topic with which we began, that of attitudes. Earlier we looked at the right attitudes to the sales process, now we look at the attitudes you bring to bear closer in, in terms of your deployment of the many methods and techniques involved. Look at it all in the way most likely to get you operating in the best possible manner and make clients feel you are a professional person to do business with, and your sales may well increase.

Adopt a positive approach

Probably one of the oldest stories about a positive approach to selling is that which contrasts the differing attitudes of two people to a glass partially filled with water. Asked to describe it, one did so by saying that it was half empty, but the other described it as half full. It is easy to say, *be positive*, more difficult to suggest to the more pessimistic how to take such a view. A pessimist has been described as someone who thinks things are going to become much worse before they get worse. If you really think like that, perhaps you should not have a role in selling. Most people are optimistic by nature. So much so that it can be one of the reasons why certain elements of the sales task are neglected — planning and preparation being put optimistically on one side with the thought that it will all be alright on the day.

Success does, to some extent, depend on attitudes and attitudes alone. The successful person does not entertain the thought of failure, but enters every meeting convinced they can achieve the objectives. It is a question of belief. But let us consider two very practical points. First, whatever techniques of personal hype you may go in for, there are a number of tangible factors from which this kind of positive attitude flows and many of them are topics of their own within this book. For example, you will be more confident of success if you:

- Know your clients and your product/service.
- Prepare.
- Anticipate your clients' reactions.

So think about what does help you in your kind of business and make a mental note to use it in how you approach the process of winning business.

Second, you must *sound* positive. Clients notice anything less and will read it as a lack of certainty about the claims you make for your product. You should be saying:

- This *will* be the case ...
- These *are* the reasons ...
- It *is* a ...

and not including in your conversations phrases such as:

- I think ...
- And perhaps ...
- It is possibly ...
- Maybe we could ...

Small points perhaps, but if this line is pursued consistently throughout your conversation, then the client will see you as authoritative, having the courage of your convictions and believe you are setting out for them what you clearly believe and are prepared to demonstrate is the case.

Selling demands a positive approach, you operate better if you are thinking positively and you will come over in a better light to those with whom you deal. This is true; positively so.

Be distinctive

Before people will buy from you, certainly on any sort of regular basis, they have to *remember* you. And often professional people all appear similar and it is rather difficult to differentiate in either appearance or manner. There is, as a result, advantage in standing out, although you do have to be careful about doing so with inappropriate gimmicks. There are some people who appear to get away with outrageous gimmicks, but they have to be good to do so.

Some seem to make it work. I have met people who always wore a bright bow tie, had oversize pink spectacle frames, wore a distinctive hat, drove an antique convertible Bentley or always wrote everything in a fountain pen filled with green ink, although I would not recommend unthinking copying in this sort of area. What works for someone else may be disaster for you, although if you have your own version of this and it works, do not let this put you off.

There is another approach to creating this necessary memorability, however, which bases a point of distinction on something more practical. For example, a friend told me of being taken to view a house by someone who (presumably with the permission of the owner who was absent) produced tea, coffee and doughnuts for him and his wife to eat as they sat on the patio on a summer's day; not a bad way of lengthening the time they spent there and increasing the feel they got of the place.

Now that is creative thinking. It creates distinction, yet does so in context of the objectives, the way the business works and, not least, in a manner the client approves. If you can think of ways that meet these criteria and that help you stand out, then you may become better remembered and be so for what are considered the right reasons. It does pay to stand out.

Ride out failure

The English actor and playwright Noel Coward once said (of a fellow writer): *That poor man. He's completely unspoiled by failure.* As he said it, he doubtless intended it as an insult, but there is a germ of a good motto there for most of us involved in selling. Failure — a client who says a firm, No — is likely to be something that occurs regularly. In some kinds of selling, the anticipated and actual failure rate is high; (the highest I have come across was 99% a level that still allowed profitable operation). Certainly in the property world it should not be anything like so high, and whatever your business there will be a prevailing strike rate.

The first thing to be clear about is simply that it happens. You will be unable to convince everyone you ever meet and there is no merit in expecting otherwise. This does not mean, of course, that you do not set out with the intention of selling to everyone. No one likes getting the negative responses. Every single one hurts, and always will; indeed, it always should. But that should not mean that you go into a fit of depression after receiving a, No, and it most certainly does not mean that you allow your next meeting to be reduced in effectiveness because you are extra worried about it.

You need to come to terms with the ratios. Every new contact has a chance of success. The job is to work in such a way that those chances are increased. On the other hand, some, inevitably, will not result in firm business and a few will result in an ego bruising brush off, and occasionally real rudeness. Never mind, it is best to regard this as going with the territory, as they say.

A run of negative results is difficult to take, but an emotional response only makes the next meeting more difficult. Analyse what went wrong by all means, think about it constructively, and make a point of learning from any identifiable mistakes. Remember too, there will not always have been a mistake; some people are never going to buy from you no matter what you do. But do not just dwell on any failure and allow yourself to become demotivated by it; confidence in what you do is important and you must not let this valuable commodity evaporate in a fit of anger or regret at one meeting that does not pan out the way you want.

Learn to bounce back from the misses and you will keep the strike rate up; and reduce the stress levels as well.

Be confident

It is easy to say, *be confident*, harder sometimes to be so. In part, confidence is pure belief in yourself, and, as such, you are the only person who can cultivate it. But confidence is also a matter of preparation (which has been mentioned) and experience.

Consider preparation first. There are many aspects of this that should raise your confidence, for instance, if you:

- Know your product/service.
- Know the client and have done some research.
- Have set clear objectives.
- Have thought through the kind of meeting you want to run.
- Have anticipated objections that may be raised.

- Prepare any necessary supporting sales aids for the meeting.

Prepare these factors and more, and the certainty that follows that some of the variables involved are no longer quite so unpredictable will bolster your confidence.

Not everything, and sometimes not very much, is predictable. Here experience comes in: you know you have a capacity to deal with most of the kinds of things that may occur. If you have been in a sales role for a while there is not so much that occurs that is totally new. Everything comes in unique form from the individuals who are your contacts and clients, but you know you have a facility for dealing with the various permutations. And you know (I hope) that you learn from experience, every meeting you have, every client you talk to, should make you just a little more able to cope with the next and the next after that. Again, all this is a source of confidence. Look for and use the things that are around that can increase your confidence and, while avoiding bravado or over reliance on technical prowess, which can stifle thought and consideration, approach every situation with the fullest confidence you can muster. Being confident is a habit. It can give you the edge on any competitor who, while perhaps as well qualified, is more hesitant about their ability to do what is necessary to succeed.

Learn from experience

An attitude that prompts you to learn from experience is valuable in any activity where you strive for excellence. In winning business it is a very real asset. Selling, as has been referred to previously, is a dynamic activity, yet it can have a repetitive element (how many times do you say whatever follows, *Let me tell you something about the firm ...?* It is easy to get into a rut and find you are repeating all the ways you have developed — even the exact words — regardless of whether they remain valid or not. This tendency to repetition can be made more likely by the way clients behave. It is said that selling is a skill that can literally get worse with practice. As clients respond, any negative tone to their response tends to lead to a dilution of sales effort as people tend to play it safe, opting for what is least likely to upset clients rather than for what will be most likely to convince them.

On the other hand, as you meet clients you have the opportunity to build up experience in a marked way. Every meeting potentially holds surprises, opportunities to experiment and learn from the way things go. This means watching for things that are not quite as you would wish, and also noting those things that go well so that they can be repeated and developed further.

This approach must be maintained. You must never be complacent and believe that you know all about selling and do not have to worry about it any more. Everyone in selling spends a lifetime learning about it, refining it and adapting what they do to present and future conditions. The right attitude to this makes possible the fine-tuning that keeps approaches fresh and maximises there effectiveness; also it makes the sales role more rewarding, more likely to produce the results you want — and more fun.

Plan ahead

What of the future? The process of persuading clients to do business with you is likely to become increasingly complex as the market and individual client attitudes change. You will have a fair idea of what makes for success in your business at present, and of what causes the difficulties. Let us review the key elements.

Selling is a form of communication, albeit persuasive communication. Good professionals are good communicators and those skills need to be kept in good order. But research and preparation are important too. "Doing your homework" can be a differentiating factor and time must always be built in for doing it. Successful approaches are based on client needs, so you need to be able to find out successfully what your clients want and why, then you can match needs with benefits and sell on that basis, providing proof and evidence as necessary along the way. You must be able to handle objections, rebalancing the argument as you go along, and you must close — aim every time for a commitment from the client that either secures the business or moves matters constructively forward.

You may also need less fundamental skills, account analysis and planning may be vital in your business, or major accounts or large individual orders may necessitate more sophisticated account handling and development skills. Other skills may be needed:

- To be equally persuasive in writing, with proposals or quotations.
- High financial competence or negotiating skills; to be as effective and persuasive when on your feet presenting in front of a group as you are one to one across a desk.

- To be expert at recognising real potential in prospects or excellent at cross-selling a range of products.
- To be able to work productively and effectively.

There are no "magic formulae". But of two things you can be sure; first, the mix of skills that are necessary to success will change and second, those who recognise the changing demands on them first will steal a march on their less predictive competitors.

This section shows that success in winning business is influenced by a whole raft of things, some apparently intangible — the way you think and how you approach things. Whatever way your business is going it pays to be looking and planning ahead, watching for changes should ensure you see them coming, expecting to change will make it easier to do so.

Part 5

Afterword —
the Way Ahead

The qualities that I believe make a good salesman:

- Believe in your product.
- Believe in yourself.
- See plenty of people.
- Pay attention to timing.
- Listen to the customer — but realise that what the customer wants is not necessarily what he or she is telling you.
- Develop a sense of humour.
- Knock on old doors.
- Ask everyone to buy.
- Follow up after the sale with the same aggressiveness you demonstrated in the sale.
- Use common sense.

I have no illusions that I am breaking new ground with this list. These are essential, self-evident, universal qualities that all sales people know in their heads — if not in their hearts.

Mark H McCormack

Afterword — the Way Ahead

A salesman has to use his imagination, deliberately and consciously, to think up just what little things he can do to be helpful to each customer. Every case calls for different tactics. That fact helps explain why aptitude testers maintain that the two traits most needed for success in selling are an objective personality and creative imagination.

Alex F Osborn, author of *Applied Imagination: Principles and Procedures of Creative Thinking* (Scribner)

In this final section, the purpose is to summarise key elements of the content of the book in a way that highlights what causes success.

If I knew one key magic formula that always guaranteed sales success I would not be writing this; I would be rich and retired. But there is, as has been said earlier, no magic formula. There are, however, a variety of things, techniques, approaches that have a disproportionately important influence on success. Some such have been mentioned throughout the text. Remember that success in winning business is largely in the detail, and that it is a fragile process. Here, without intending to sideline other issues, key aspects of what makes for success in selling in the property areas on which this book focuses are reviewed under 10 main headings.

1. Selling is part of marketing

Sales activity must not take place in isolation. It is an inherent part of marketing. Thus, people charged with the sales role must:

- Recognise that clients see, and experience, sales in this way. For example, they may know something of an organisation ahead of a sales meeting (from promotion and advertising, among other things); they may have checked out competitors, visited a number of websites and more. They expect what happens through the contact and communications that take place to reflect, maintain and extend any good image that may have been projected initially. They expect specific promises made through other media to be kept. If your website tells people, *A half hour briefing will give you all you need* — then it must do just that.
- Act and talk in a way that gels well with other activities and messages.

This presupposes that marketing activity is conducted in a way that sees personal selling as an integral part of the way the organisation interrelates with its clients. So advertising and promotion may need to reflect the fact that prospective clients will need to see someone face-to-face as part of the process that is necessary if they are to make a sensible buying decision. Mismatch here just causes problems and jeopardises potential sales. If you promise someone further information, contact their office to prompt the action and then there is a delay, the potential client will see this as an inefficiency of both the person and the organisation, and one that does not bode well for the quality of service to follow.

If you wear the sales hat, you have a responsibility to spot any such occurrences (and they can come from many areas) and communicate about them to ensure they are corrected. Good management is alert to such intelligence and will ensure that things run smoothly and that nothing is allowed to dilute sales effectiveness.

2. Selling must be client-orientated

Selling, to repeat, is not something that you do to people. It is an interactive process that must, as much as anything, reflect the client end of the relationship. This means specifically that:

- Peoples' needs must be accurately identified. Only if you know what their situation (it might be a problem or an opportunity) is, can you address it. Moreover, if you address it better than competitors, then this is the best method of differentiating yourself and your organisation.

- Sales approaches must respect the individual on the other end. Are they experienced, knowledgeable (or not), are they worried or confident? Conversations must not just incorporate such information and do so specifically, but also *be seen* to do so. Displayed empathy scores points.
- A sales approach, especially in selling bespoke services, must not appear standardised. People must feel you are interested in them, addressing their specific situation and that what you say is *for them*, not just what you always say to everyone.

A conscious focus on the client will help direct the entire communication in the right kind of way, giving it bite and giving it an edge.

3. Selling must reflect the buying process

This picks up from point two. Here what is advocated is not a general client orientation but a reflection of the whole process that a client is going through in making a decision. In the same way that in boxing or judo you "go with the attack", here you will do better following the client's inclinations (although perhaps modifying and imparting particular emphasis to them), rather than fighting against them. The thinking process set out earlier really does constitute an effective basis on which to proceed. If you get out of kilter with a prospect, then they will not only not see the relevance of what you are saying, but also they will resent it.

When I changed my car recently I talked to three dealers (looking at cars in broadly the same bracket). I was not asked a single question by any of them. Amazing! How can you sell a car if you do not know whether the potential buyer is married, has children or a dog, how many miles they drive in a year and more? I was offered plenty of information, but it lacked any credibility — it was the standard spiel. This is a dramatic example, from another sector, but makes a good point. The logic dictates that the customer expects to be asked questions, and for the presentation to be based on the answers. Any aspect of the client's buying process that is ignored risks failure and the likelihood that what they want will be better satisfied elsewhere.

4. Selling demands preparation

You cannot wing it. Even the best and most experienced professional people rarely wing it (although they may make it look a little like they do). Success comes from sound preparation. The first rule is simple — *you always prepare*. What actually needs to be done, however, may vary considerably.

You may only need a couple of quiet minutes before going into someone's office. You may need to sit down with one or two colleagues for a couple of hours to thrash out the best way ahead. You may not be able to prepare (as say when you meet someone by chance and the transaction is immediately under way). In the latter case, you still need to be prepared: you can think in advance about the type(s) of transaction that may occur and be ready for most of them.

You may need to make notes, you may need alternative strategies, or you may want to rehearse (for a major sale). You *do* need to do something. Consider exactly what is necessary in every situation, do it and you automatically increase your chances of success. You cannot predict exactly what will happen, you still need to be quick on your feet, but you will be better able to cope with whatever may come your way if you are prepared.

5. Selling must be delivered in an appropriate manner

Selling in the property sector (especially the services side of it) needs a soft approach: one *not* lacking in persuasive power, but not weak either. The power — projection — that you bring to bear is important. You need confidence, authority even; certainly people must believe you have the position, personality and profile to be credible in your role.

Empathy is the other key attribute. You need to see things from other peoples' point of view and *be seen to do so*. Good empathy balances the powerful approach you want to bring to bear, it softens sales techniques that would otherwise be seen as "hard sell" and makes what you do acceptable as well as appropriate.

This is especially important when there is an element of advice inherent in what you are doing; and there is in many property situations from selling planning advice to architectural services. Advice must seem soundly based. It must not simply and obviously be what you want and what is best for you. The right blend here is worth working at. Think about how your client might best want you to match their expectations to some extent. Do not leave out the edge you want, but remember that if what you do is unacceptable it will quickly be rejected as someone moves on to a competitor.

6. Selling must incorporate effective need identification

Selling is not just about telling — describing — things to people. Success has at least as much to do with asking questions. So:

- Think about areas to question and plan how to phrase matters clearly (not least so that you can obtain the information you want quickly and the process does not become like the Spanish Inquisition).
- Establish and agree that questioning is necessary (you do not want it to distract or worry people — the logic of the approach should be clear).
- Listen to, and note if necessary, the answers.

Then your proposition can be tailored around their exact situation. The principle here is the same whether the circumstances only permit a couple of quick questions or if you can take half an hour to establish details or confirm (or revise) the brief, as it would be for, say, a surveyor, that is: what they want, and why they want it. Always good needs identification puts you in a position to make a stronger, and better targeted, pitch and differentiate yourself and your organisation more easily from competition.

7. Selling must use memorable and creative description

There is a danger with selling that what is said becomes routine, repetitive and dull. You may find that you start to abbreviate a little (because you have heard it all before) and the best possible case is no longer made.

There are principles to be followed here:

- Remember that unexpected clarity (especially if something is expected to be complicated) delights people — you need to communicate and, with services especially, to ignite peoples' imagination. This is a real opportunity to shine (and to differentiate).

- Think about the best way of putting things, and do not let the way you talk about something become stale.
- Keep what you say up to date, correct and fresh and make sure it is in "the clients' language" (and remember too much inappropriate jargon can deaden any description).
- Bring it to life. Avoid bland language — nothing you offer is just *quite* (or even *very*) *good* — and avoid imprecise words such as *flexible* that attempt to be descriptive and fail (what does flexible mean? If you are reading this book you will notice that this page is flexible). Work at a description to create something clear and memorable. Consider a general phrase: to describe something as *sort of shiny* (wet fish?). It is better to say it is *as smooth a silk* (which certainly conjures up a more precise image), and better still — and more unmistakable and memorable — to say that it is *as slippery as a freshly buttered ice rink*.

Language is the most powerful personal tool you can use in winning business; use it in a well-considered way to get the most from it.

8. Selling must be benefit-led

The concept of benefits and features, was investigated earlier and I will not return to the details here. Suffice to say that this is a crucial aspect of successful property selling; and something that, again, can enhance differentiation and do so positively. Always you must be:

- Clear what the specific benefits of an offering are and able to differentiate them from features (something that needs a little thought and is not quite as obvious as may be thought at first sight).
- Able to prioritise and describe benefits appropriately in light of what is known about a particular client. Remember a benefit is a benefit, but not all benefits are relevant to every buyer (money saved is certainly always "a benefit", but cheapest is not always best and for some people intent on maximising quality it may not be a relevant benefit).
- Able to make benefits predominate in the overall conversation and relate what they do to the overall "weighing up" process that characterises the way people buy.

Benefits should mostly come first — tell people what they get, then use features to demonstrate how this is possible. This, coupled with the powers of description mentioned in point 7 in this summary, makes for a powerful approach at the core of the sales process.

9. Selling is a complex process and must be managed

The biggest challenge of selling is perhaps in the management of the whole process. Each individual stage is essentially manageable. But there can be a great deal going on. Throughout a meeting you have to follow your plan and deal with anything leading you away from it. You need to fine-tune what you are doing to accommodate unanticipated factors along the way (and to do that you have to notice them!). You must listen, concentrate and judge how you do things as well as what you will do. You must draw with precision from a not inconsiderable body of information about your offering, clients, industry and more, much of which must be held in your head. And all this must take place alongside whatever technical expertise your work involves.

Understanding what needs to be done is important here; the people best at winning business exhibit a real awareness of the details of the sales process and how it works. So too is confidence, for example you may need to have sufficient confidence to say *I don't know* or pause and say *Let me think about that for a moment* (a much better option than jumping in with an ill-considered answer, although it can be awkward to do it).

Beyond this, what helps? Practice. Remember the anecdote mentioned early about golfers, practice and luck. Selling is a skill we can spend a lifetime in learning. It is dynamic and so is the environment in which property businesses operate. Recognise that and you are half way to dealing with it.

10. Effectively selling must take a long-term view

Success may follow a quick meeting followed by a clear agreement. That is nice, but it is certainly not always what happens. As you sell you have to keep the longer-term view in mind. Let me suggest two degrees of time-scale that need to be contemplated:

- *The immediate aftermath of a meeting*: This is best illustrated by the occasion when interest seems high, but you cannot get past a *Leave it with me* comment. Here persistence pays off. Keep in touch, arrange to contact them again and do so as many times as it takes. It is easy to lose heart as you telephone and are given excuses. Ask when a meeting finishes, contact them again and ring the changes in terms of method — telephone, write, fax, e-mail. If there really is no prospect they will tell you, while there might be possibilities of business, you need to remain fresh in their mind, not a competitor. Increased persistence can be an easy, low-cost way of boosting sales.
- *Long-term contact*: After a sale is successfully made (or not, when it may still be worth re-contacting people) make a plan of ongoing contact and avoid losing touch. Seek recommendations, plan a client strategy, analyse the nature especially of large client organisations. As has been said, it is easier and less expensive to obtain more business from those who you know, who have worked with you in the past and found this satisfactory, than to seek out new, but cold, prospects. Nurture what you have; it can pay dividends in the future.

A final word

It is difficult, perhaps deceiving, to try to encapsulate briefly a topic such as selling, however I am confident that these 10 points make sense. Especially in selling intangible services the details of the matter become even more important, and what can be gained by careful use of core techniques and of approaches that affect things in key ways is considerable.

This review sets out specific techniques and also highlights other matters: approaches and attitudes that affect matters along the way. What is needed here is that such are:

- Grafted onto the stock in trade expertise that you use in your particular field of the property world to work along side that, enhancing the overall approach rather than replacing it.
- Used in such a way that clients continue to see the relationship you intend to forge as truly professional.
- Applied on a bespoke basis: so that what is done is always tailored client-by-client and meeting-by-meeting to the individual circumstances of each case.

Many property professional people initially baulk at the thought of selling — *I'm a professional, I can't be pushy.* Many also, in my experience, once they set their mind to it (and competitive markets make that a logical option), find that sales techniques can go comfortably alongside their professionalism. They find that their professionalism is enhanced, and that so too are the results that they achieve in securing and developing profitable business.

It is always satisfying when new business is secured, and the driver for this may be simple: just a recommendation and a good image may be sufficient in some cases, and we would be lost if some business was not won comparatively easily. But most needs more and it is even more satisfying when new business is secured and you can look back, sometimes at a long complex chain of events, and say, *I made that happen.*

Now, hopefully with some ideas drawn from here in mind, I wish you well with it.

Index